# COLLAGE,
# APPLIQUE AND PATCHWORK
## — a practical guide

Anne Coleman

Bishopsgate Press Ltd.,
Bartholomew House, 15 Tonbridge Road,
Hildenborough, Kent, TN11 9BH

Cover picture: *Colour Change 11* by Christine Cooper

All enquiries and requests relevant to this title should be sent to the publisher, Bishopsgate Press Ltd., Bartholomew House, 15 Tonbridge Road, Hildenborough, Kent, TN11 9BH

Printed in Great Britain by
Whitstable Litho Printers Ltd., Whitstable, Kent

# Contents

I hope this book will give just some idea of the potential for using fabric in a creative way. The basic methods and techniques are easy, but with the variety of available fabrics and simple hand-printing techniques, the possibilities are endless.

If you feel something will work, do not be afraid to try it out and experiment. There is no doubt that individual choice of colour and tone, composition and pattern, gives an enormous amount of personal satisfaction.

We live in an age of communication. Standards are high because we are able to see experts on TV and in magazines and books. However, the majority of people who are interested in textiles have neither the time nor the inclination to be high-powered, but nevertheless get enormous satisfaction from using fabrics in a creative way.

Embroiderers' Guild Groups and Quilters' Guilds throughout the country are not only for experts, but for those who are interested and want to learn more. These groups, and adult education classes welcome people who want to have the chance to see and try new ideas and meet others with similar interests.

We are are lucky to be able to practise a craft for recreation and pleasure and should take full advantage of all that is on offer.

Anne Coleman
1992

# Acknowledgments

I would like to thank all those who helped me in the preparation of this book, particularly Roberta Warren, for invaluable assistance and advice. Many thanks to all the people who have allowed me to include photographs of their own work. Thanks also to Maureen Cox, Edith Holliday and Shirley Gibb for allowing me to reproduce photographs of pieces belonging to them.

The photographs on pages 37 and 71 are reproduced by kind permission of The American Museum in Britain, Claverton Manor, Bath.

I would like to thank Peter Coleman for taking photographs and giving much encouragement and support.

# Introduction

Fabric is an essential commodity throughout the world and is used to create clothing and furnishings. However, human beings seem to have a basic need to add decoration, and change something which might otherwise be rather dull and functional into something exciting and unique.

People have always used up their spare bits of fabric to patch holes, and using a piece of cloth cut in a practical shape is only one step from making a succession of fancy shapes or a picture for its own sake. This thrifty desire to use up scraps of fabric in a decorative way is probably how appliqué and patchwork evolved.

Fabric collage, appliqué and patchwork are all aspects of piecing together fabric shapes to create a picture or a pattern. In collage, fabrics are stuck rather than sewn. In appliqué, fabric pieces are applied to a background with stitches. Patchwork is a complete fabric made by sewing together smaller pieces often, but not always, in the form of geometric shapes.

All art should be a reflection of its own time, not a copy of the past, but growing from it and evolving into something new. In our own society where all types of embroidery are done to make a personal statement and the lines between the techniques are often blurred, experimentation with fabrics and threads is positively encouraged. Creating the colour and pattern on the fabric used in a project, and using fabrics and papers to plan designs, make the finished work more individual and give a chance of self-expression. The choice of fabric is of particular importance, and many technically excellent pieces of work have no visual impact because the various fabrics do not show one another to best advantage. Because of this, it is important that the design and colour scheme are carefully thought out before starting.

Of all embroidery techniques, appliqué and patchwork can still be used in a functional as well as a pictorial way. They are often used for large artefacts like hangings, banners, flags and ecclesiastical embroidery because it is easy to get a quick but dramatic and theatrical effect. Where appliqué is used in a purely decorative way, unusual and interesting fabrics which might not previously have been considered can be used.

The first part of this book is about collecting, colouring and patterning fabrics and using them directly to experiment with colour, pattern and shape. The second is about creating designs, and some common techniques of patchwork and appliqué.

# TOOLS AND EQUIPMENT

We live in an age of all-pervading technology, yet traditional crafts are based on very simple equipment. A needle, some scissors and some pieces of scrap fabrics are all that is really needed for patchwork and appliqué.

The following list can be gradually assembled as each item becomes really necessary.

## Needles

Choose needles which are comfortable to use and the right size for your thread. Sharp needles are best for sewing fabrics together, and needles with a round rather than a long eye hold the thread without slipping. Blunt or tapestry needles are for embroidery where the needle goes between rather than through the threads of the fabric.

If you find a needle difficult to thread, try a needle threader. You will find that needle threading improves with practice. Use the smallest needle you can manage. — generally size 9 or 10.

A thimble helps you to push the needle through several layers of fabric with ease. Wear it on the middle finger of the hand you use to hold the needle.

## Scissors

Sharp scissors are essential for any work which involves cutting fabric accurately. Keep a pair of scissors for textiles only, and another separate pair for cutting paper.

## Stitch rippers

These are useful for starting off an awkward piece of cutting out. They are sharp, so be careful not to cut too much by mistake.

## Pins

Dressmakers stainless steel pins will last well if they are stored in their tin or box.

Glass headed pins are useful for pinning out fabric and paper shapes, although the coloured heads can be distracting.

## Tweezers

A good pair of tweezers is excellent for placing pieces of fabric without upsetting the surrounding arrangement.

## Softboard

A piece of softboard can be used for pinning out chosen fabrics so that they can be viewed together and seen from a distance. The board can also be utilised for pinning out fabric to be printed and for arranging and rearranging patchwork shapes.

## FRAMES

Embroidery frames are particularly good for appliqué where the work has to be held flat. The frame acts like a table and it is easy to keep the pieces in position while sewing. Some large frames have their own stand, but it is quite convenient to balance one edge of a smaller frame on a table and the opposite edge on the back of a chair. Both hands are free and can then be used to sew. Some frames have a clamp which can be attached to a chair arm or the edge of a table.

**Specialist embroidery frames, floor frames and slate frames.** These can be obtained in various sizes from textile craft suppliers, by mail order or from large haberdashery departments. They usually comprise two bars covered with canvas strip and two bars which act as spacers. Before the background fabric is attached to the frame, it should be strengthened by turning in a hem and machining all the way round.

Attaching the background fabric to a frame is called "dressing the frame". Oversew the top and bottom hem to the canvas strips. Use thin

*Dressed floor frame*

7

twine to stitch round the spacers at each side so the fabric is taut but not distorted.

**Canvas stretchers**

These are available from art suppliers. They are sold separately and come in a variety of lengths which can be slotted together at the corners to form a rectangle of suitable size.

The background fabric should always have a spare border of fabric all the way round, then the work can be pinned through this onto the frame with drawing pins. Canvas stretchers are comparatively cheap, and easy to set up.

If a useful frame is too big for a particular piece of work, dress the frame with a piece of calico or cotton and sew the work onto it. Sew through both fabrics.

**Tambour rings**

It is often easier to work on a small scale, eventually assembling the finished pieces to create a larger piece.

Round embroidery hoops or rings are sold in several sizes and are useful for these small pieces of work. Some are made of wood, some of plastic. The frame will hold a background fabric more securely if the inside ring is bound with bias binding.

A larger quilting hoop is available from specialist suppliers.

Flat plastic rings with a sprung inner ring are useful for machine embroidery.

**Iron**

This is essential, as fabrics need to be pressed at all stages in the course of the work. Bonding materials are also very useful and these are ironed on. An iron is used to set fabric colours and make them fast. A cleaner for the base of the iron is available from hardware suppliers.

**THE SEWING-MACHINE**

Appliqué and many types of patchwork can be done by machine or by hand, or by using a combination of both methods. Any sewing-machine is suitable, including hand machines and treadles, provided it is in good working order.

Get to know your sewing-machine by reading the Instruction Manual carefully.

Learn how to thread the needle and the bobbin.

Try the machine out on spare fabric, then look at the back of the sewing to make sure the tension is correct. If it is not, the Instruction Manual will advise you on how to alter it.

Learn how to adjust the tension on both the top and bottom thread.

Sometimes it is necessary to take the machine to a supplier who will show you how to adjust it, or it might need to be mended. Many old machines need a small adjustment by an expert, and a good supplier can often give advice. Often a machine only needs a good clean and some oil.

A machine which does not work properly is no use to anyone.

It is worth spending several hours getting the feel of the machine. This can be done in a constructive way by making patterned or textured fabrics. These fabrics can then be used in appliqué or patchwork.

Use a variety of different types of fabric about 20cm square like calico, silk, velvet, translucent fabric and felt etc., to see how each reacts to stitching.

Make even and uneven stripes and criss-cross patterns from one side of the fabric to the other, using both straight and satin stitch. Fancy patterns can be used in conjunction with straight lines. Start at the edge of the fabric and sew across, finishing at the opposite edge. Cut off surplus threads.

Making tucks and pleats also gives texture. and these fabrics will also come in useful for patchwork and appliqué. (see p.25)

Many people are very tentative with their sewing-machine, yet it is a robust piece of equipment and will not break easily.

Straight stitch can be used for joining patches. Lines of machine stitches can also be used to attach applied shapes, but it you want to make more intricate turns and swirls, learn to do free machine embroidery. You can do this on all except hand-operated machines.

**Free machine embroidery or DARNING**   The machine works because the feed or teeth in the base of the machine and the presser foot pull the fabric through the machine automatically.

When the machine is set up for darning or free embroidery, these facilities are disconnected and the machine sews on the spot.

*Landscape. Applied fringe and cut out flowers. Machine embroidered*

Remove the presser foot (not the bar). Lower the feed. On many machines, this is done by pressing a button. Some machines have a plate to cover the feed. Look for the method for your machine in the Instruction Manual.

The fabric must be held flat and taut in some way, otherwise the machine will pull it out of shape. This can be done by:

1.  Using a frame. Machine embroidery frames come in several sizes, but the smaller sizes are easier to begin with. Hold the frame like a saucer and keep it flat on the base plate. The frame is moved from one area to another as you work.
2.  Use a stiff background fabric. This might be:
    a)  Paper backed fabric (wallcovering)
    b)  You can make paper backed fabric by pasting paper with diluted PVA glue. Stick fabric to this, ironing on the paper side, so the two materials bond together.
    c)  Fabric dipped in wallpaper paste and left to dry.
    d)  Starched fabric.
    e)  Fabric backed with iron-on interfacing.
    The important point to keep in mind is that the fabric is held flat in some way. The fabric should stay flat on the base plate at all times.
    Machine needles are available in several sizes and for different materials.
    Use a sharp machine needle to suit the fabric you are using. A heavier needle is necessary if you are using paper or several layers of fabric.
1.  Put the needle bar in the DOWN position. Bring the bottom thread to the top and hold both threads to one side.
2.  Sew evenly, gently pushing the ring with the fingers and keeping it flat.
    Make small patterns like circles and spirals.
    Practise for a short time every day and use the time to create fabrics with a texture or a pattern of stitches, trying out a variety of different fabrics,threads and stitches.

## MACHINE THREAD

There are many different machine threads, including metallic threads, machine embroidery threads in both plain and graduated colours as well as thicker top threads.

Always use the same weight of thread in the bobbin and the needle to maintain an even tension.

## WORKING SPACE

Textiles can take a lot of space, but with some ingenuity it is possible to work in a very small area.

An alcove, even an understairs cupboard or a standing cupboard can be turned into a viable working area and storage space.

Make use of racks which fit under shelves. A trestle table, even an old door on trestles or between two smaller tables, can be stored standing

*Applied fabric on paper backed hessian.*

vertical. Wallpaper tables can be folded up into a small space. A wide shelf could be hinged, to hang down when not in use.

Plastic stacking boxes, shoe boxes, plastic sandwich boxes can all be used for storage, and plastic or drawstring bags and baskets can be hung behind doors or on hooks under shelves.

Many DIY stores have all kinds of storage boxes and containers, plastic cisterns, stacking boxes etc., and it is worth looking round to see what might be utilised. Plastic sweet jars, for example are very useful for storing either fabric scraps or threads.

The smaller the space, the more important it is to label boxes.

Try to work in a good light. An angle lamp is useful because it can be used to light a particular area. It can also be used by an individual person who wants to work while others are watching TV. Daylight bulbs are available.

# PLANNING AND DESIGN

Patchwork is a very easy technique. However, a piece can be improved dramatically by using the right colour tones. Similarly, it is well worth going to a lot of trouble to find just the right piece of fabric to fit in an appliqué picture.

The components of design are colour and texture, and pattern and shape. In a good design these must work together to give the impression you want to create.

People who spend time researching in these areas to get exactly the right effect, find the experience both rewarding and enjoyable. In addition these experiments often lead to ideas for future pieces of work.

Planning and designing a piece of work is easier if you have some relevant basic equipment to work with and there are several useful and easy methods of creating patterns and pictures.

## MARKERS AND COLOUR

Pencils, felt-tips, pens, crayons, all make different marks. People are all individual and enjoy using particular types of pencils, pens and colouring media, and there are many to choose from.

Look round your own environment and you will probably be able to find quite a number of markers: pencils, pens, felt-tips and children's wax and plastic crayons, perhaps even a small paintbox. These make the nucleus of the collection.

Walk round an artists' suppliers or a craft shop and notice what is available. Try samples where you can. Look at markers in different sizes, pencils from hard to very soft, dip pens, fibre-tipped pens and ball-points.

Notice the numbers of different paints and colouring media, poster and watercolour paints, oil and pastels, coloured markers etc.

Markers come in all colours and it would be enormously expensive to purchase sets of everything, so obtain just one or two at a time in a colour you like, perhaps a thick marker, a thin fibre-tip and a charcoal pencil to give a variety of line.

It is a good idea to have one medium (HB) and one soft (4B) pencil for drawing and one hard (2H) for drawing geometric shapes on fabric or paper.

A fabric marker which makes a water dissolvable mark can be bought in the haberdashery department of most large stores.

Add to your collection gradually, trying before buying wherever possible.

## PAPER

*Graph paper.* Interlocking patterns can be designed on graph paper and ordinary SQUARE graph paper or dressmakers' graph paper is readily available. ISOMETRIC graph paper, based on a network of triangles can be obtained from many large stationers. Both types are used for designing patterns for patchwork.

There are also some interesting books of interlocking patterns which can be used to plan designs. (Altair)

*square graph paper*

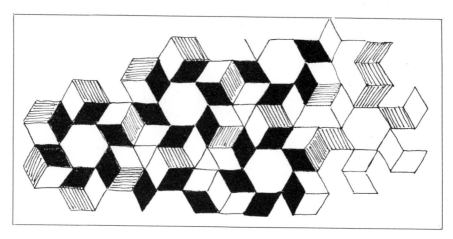

*isometric graph paper*

Coarse *sandpaper* is used in conjuction with graph paper to make patchwork templates (see p56).

*Tracing paper:* This is essential for tracing templates for appliqué. Graph paper marked with a grid pattern is also available. *Greaseproof paper* is not only a cheap alternative, but can be used for transfer fabric printing.

*Paper for templates:* Make a collection of strong firm paper, brown paper, used envelopes or writing paper to make patchwork templates.

There are many other useful and interesting papers available in all colours ranging from brown wrapping paper to exotic handmade papers, beautifully coloured or marbled. Look round a large stationers or an art and craft shop.

*Cartridge paper,* coloured drawing paper and sugar paper are all useful as background for sticking and for drawing.

Coloured *tissue paper* is translucent and can be overlaid to produce other colours. *Wrapping paper,* both patterned and metallic can be cut and stuck, and more pattern can be added to commercially patterned paper.

The packets of *sticky-backed paper* and cut-out shapes sold in toy shops give shiny textures and bright colours. Quite large areas of colour can be cut from magazines. Keep the pieces together in colour groups in a plastic envelope.

Cheap *wallpaper* and lining paper are not only useful for planning large designs, but also for colouring and for cutting and tearing patterns.

*Blotting paper,* kitchen paper and paper hankies are soft and absorbent, and can be used for dabbing paint or for tearing and glueing as well as to make smudgy painted effects.

Because so many colours are available and paper is expensive, it is a good idea to begin by buying dark, medium and light tones of just one colour as well as black, grey and white.

## MAKING PATTERNS

Try out crayons and other markers on small squares (approx 15cm x 15cm) of a variety of different papers to see how each reacts.

Make lines of criss-cross patterns, filling in some of the areas between. Use straight, wavy and zigzag lines.

Scribble or hatch lines to make texture, or use a sponge or screwed up paper, dipped in paint.

Keep the hand-patterned papers to use when designing patchwork and appliqué and use the same techniques for fabric printing and painting.

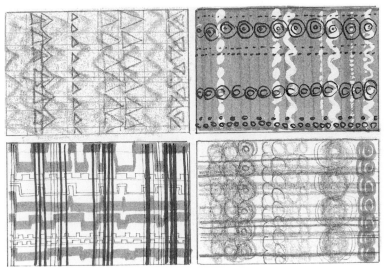

*Patterns on paper with various colouring media.*

## OTHER EQUIPMENT

Patchwork and appliqué involve accurate measuring and cutting out. A steel ruler is more expensive than plastic or wood, but it will last longer and the edges will not deteriorate.

Craft knives and rotary cutters can be obtained at art and ironmongers shops and DIY stores.

It is possible to obtain a self-healing cutting board with measurements marked out. Although these are comparatively expensive, they are excellent for measuring and cutting. A vinyl tile can be used as a cheap alternative.

A pair of compasses is useful and blackboard dividers can be used for large-scale work.

## GLUE

Use glues which are compatible with paper as well as fabrics. These are usually water-based, like PVA and wallpaper paste, or spirit-based like Copydex and Spray Mount.

Always use as little glue as possible and read the instructions carefully as some glues need to be applied to both surfaces and or need to dry for a few minutes before sticking.

It is almost always easier to spread the glue on the background surface and place the pieces on it, using a pair of tweezers. Allow glued areas to dry thoroughly.

Where wallpaper paste is used to stick fabrics, dip the fabric in the paste until it is soaked. Scrape off the excess, then smooth onto the background and leave to dry. Mix the paste according to the instructions.

## OTHER RESOURCES

Always keep notes of past experiments so that discoveries can be repeated. Do not throw away try-outs and bits of experimental material.

A great number of patterns are universal and can also be seen in ornament on wood and metal, stone and ceramics and other materials. It is useful to collect and copy these patterns in a notebook. Photographs, postcards and cuttings, experiments and designs can all be kept in plastic envelopes and stored in a ring binder.

Use a scrap-book or simply tuck pictures, pieces of fabric and thread in the cheap photograph albums with clear pull-back sheets.

A small sketch-book with a spiral ring-binder is useful for writing notes and drawing small sketches. Alternatively, pages can be added to a personal organiser. Cut a selection of different papers including cartridge paper, and punch holes down the side. Intersperse these with lined paper for notes.

Write down or sketch interesting patterns, colour schemes and textures. Record ideas that occur at odd moments and would otherwise be forgotten.

It is difficult to carry a range of coloured pencils or paints, but make a list of colours with scraps of coloured paper, paint samples or scraps of coloured fabrics and number these. If you need to note a colour, you can match it with your list.

# COLLECTING FABRICS

Fabric is familiar from earliest childhood. Quite insignificant scraps of fabric can conjure up powerful feelings and half-remembered times from the past. A collection of fabrics can be like reading an old diary.

Fabric is available in a wide range of colour and pattern and can also be coloured and printed very easily at home.

Fabrics fall into several categories, and it is useful to know what each one is, so that you will know how it will react to paint, etc.

When buying new fabric, cut off a small piece and file it in your reference book with details of fibre content. This can be important if you want to use it for something like transfer fabric printing which only uses synthetic fibres.

## 1. FIBRES

All fabrics are made from fibres which can be divided into groups.

*Natural fibres*   These are fibres from plants and from the coats of animals; cotton, linen and wool are the most well known, but there are many more.

Natural fibres are usually of a certain length (the staple length) and are spun to make a continuous thread.

Silk is a continuous thread which is wound off the cocoon of the silkworm moth.

*Man-made fibres*   Rayon viscose is made from wood pulp which is spun into a continuous thread.

*Synthetic fibres*   Yarns are made in continuous threads from petrochemicals. The filaments are either cut up and spun to copy natural fabrics or used as continuous thread.

Fabrics are made from one or a combination of different fibres, and so there is a huge and exciting array of fabrics available.  All new fabrics are labelled.

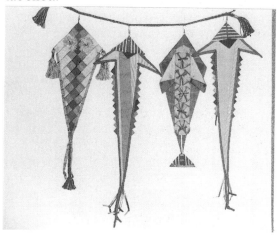

*'Fishing Line' by Alison Harding.*

17

## 2. CONSTRUCTION

Fabrics are made up in three ways.

Analyse the fabric by looking at it with a magnifying glass. A magnifier called a "little looker" is available from craft suppliers and this can be used to see the fascinating detail of different materials.

a. **Weaving**   Woven fabrics have a weft and a warp at right angles and will fray out at the edges to make a fringe. They feel firm when pulled along the weft or warp, but give when pulled on the diagonal. Traditionally, woven fabric is used for patchwork and the same fabric is used throughout (e.g all cotton, all silk, all wool). it is a good idea to stick to traditional methods for functional patchwork which is to be used and laundered. The same applies to functional appliqué where it is important that fabrics wear well and do not shrink.

In patchwork a beginner would find that cotton fabrics are easiest to manage and some people never work with anything else. Others experiment across the whole range. Both are correct. If the fabric looks right, use it.

b. **Knitting**   Knitted fabric unravels when pulled out, and is usually stretchy.Traditionally, knitted fabric is not used for patchwork or appliqué. But for decorative appliqué or experimental patchwork the choice of fabric is personal and any fabric is suitable if it gives the right effect. Knitting has an added advantage for it can be padded to create a raised effect.

c. **Felting**   Felt consists of layers of combed fibres treated with heat and water to mat the fibres together to form a fabric. Felt does not stretch or fray but will pull out of shape. Many people make felt by hand.
Felt is very useful in appliqué.

d. **Other materials**   Lengths of lace, braids, ribbons can all be used.

e. **Bonding materials**   These are made from synthetic fibres and can be used in a variety of ways.

The materials are coated with glue on one or both sides, and are activated by ironing.

*Iron-on interfacing* is made in various weights to suit different fabrics. It is useful as a support for flimsy fabrics or to stop fabric surfaces working against each other if the weave of the pieces is cut in opposite directions. It can also be used for stiffening fabric for free machine embroidery.

*Bondaweb* is adhesive on both sides, so when it is placed between fabric and background and ironed, the materials are fused together.

Packets of Bondaweb with a paper backing are sold in the haberdashery departments of chain stores.

Iron the Bondaweb to the back of the fabric you intend to use. Patterns and shapes can then be drawn on the paper backing and cut out. Peel off the paper, then iron on.

Do not allow the Bondaweb to come in contact with the bottom of the iron.
Where this is inevitable, place a piece of silicon baking parchment over the work to prevent sticking.

## 3. TEXTURE AND PATTERN

All fabrics have texture which is woven, knitted or felted into it during

18

manufacture. If you are creating a picture, this is useful and important. Look at your collection of cloth, or examine the fabrics in a dress or soft furnishing department of a store and notice the textured surfaces.

Soft fabrics like velvet and corduroy, harsher looped fabrics for upholstery and towelling, coarse open-weave curtain fabric; all have contrasting textures.

Patterns can be woven into cloth as it is being made, usually in the form of stripes, checks or plaids, as the weft and warp of the fabric make these patterns easy to achieve.

You can often fray out these fabrics quite easily to see how they are made and what colours go to make the overall colour of the fabric.

Notice the woven pattern in gingham, the variety of wool in tweed and the many different striped furnishing fabrics.

More complicated patterns are woven into fabrics like damask, and many silk and synthetic dress fabrics have a lovely self-coloured woven pattern, which changes with the light.

"Shot" fabrics are woven with one colour weft and another colour warp. Some fabrics are woven from such fine thread that they are transparent. Organza, organdie and chiffon are in this category. Notice how the colours change when one colour is placed over another.

Other fabrics are very loosely woven and easily fray out. Among these are fabrics like scrim and some furnishing fabrics, muslin and tarlatan. Look at and feel fabrics whenever you have the opportunity.

## 4. PRINTED PATTERN

A pattern might be printed on the surface of the fabric.
Patterned fabrics are used frequently in patchwork, to contrast with plain fabrics or other patterned fabrics, to produce the lovely abstract patterns which are characteristic. There is an infinite variety of printed fabrics in all combinations of colour and fibre, which is both exciting and inspiring.

As you look at fabric, make a point of trying to imagine what the fabric might be used to represent. Does it look like water, or a ploughed field, a field of flowers, the petals of a flower, blocks of windows?

Grey and dark coloured checked fabric cut in blocks might look like buildings, or layers of grey translucent fabrics like a rainy day — and so on.

## 5. SOURCES OF FABRIC AND MATERIALS

a. *Department stores*  These usually stock a selection of dress and home furnishing fabrics as well as threads. Many shops will sell in small quantities and have boxes of fabric remnants. Keep in mind the fact that fabric stocks are seasonal. Silks and satin and exotic, metallic fabrics are more likely to be available in late autumn, ready for Christmas. Printed cottons are produced in early spring. Calico, muslin, plain sheeting and interfacings are available throughout the year.

Haberdashery departments also have wide ranges of iron-on bonding materials.

b. *Specialist fabric shops*  Theatrical suppliers are often based in London, but many towns have outlets which deal exclusively in fabrics for saris. These stock a wonderful array of exotic fabrics.

Some craft shops and department stores import American fabrics specially printed for patchwork and appliqué.

c. *Mail order*  Many craft suppliers deal by post and advertise in specialist embroidery and craft magazines and sometimes in the small advertisements of women's magazines. Wholesale fabric suppliers usually take only a minimum order, but a group of like-minded friends might combine to place an order.

d. *Dressmakers*  Many people still make their own and their children's clothes and are usually quite pleased to get rid of spare pieces of fabric. Others who are also interested in creative textiles will swop pieces.

e. *Small businesses*  Those dealing in lampshade making, tailoring, making costumes for the theatre, etc. will have waste fabrics which could be just right. Look in Yellow Pages.

f. *Charity shops and jumble sales*  Look for large areas of fabric like tablecloths which might be used as background, interesting dress fabrics, felt hats, chiffon scarves,  etc. All can be washed or cleaned, and re-used.

## 6.  STORAGE

The difficulty of storing large amounts of fabric is obvious. However, fabrics can be controlled more easily if they are grouped.

Colour is one way in which fabrics can be divided, using the colours of the rainbow as a guide (red, orange, yellow, green, blue, indigo and violet). Keep black and white separate. Fabrics in colour groups like this make the collector more aware of the very fine gradations between one colour and another.

Sometimes it is useful to place plain cotton fabrics and patterned cotton fabrics into separate groups. Patterned fabric might be further sub-divided into large and small patterns.

Felt, translucent and transparent fabric such as organdie, organza and chiffon, loosely woven fabric like muslin and scrim and metallic fabric can be kept in separate groups. Laces, braids and ribbons can also be kept together.

Eventually, you will find your own method of division. The sorting out, feeling and looking at the colours, textures and patterns of fabrics is part of the fascination, and gives ideas of which fabrics look really beautiful together.

Ideally, large pieces, or several smaller pieces of similar fabric should be rolled round a card tube as this stops the fabric from creasing and marking.

However, this takes quite a lot of space, and often people have to compromise by stacking their folded fabrics so that just the edge of each fabric shows. If they have to be stacked behind one another, cut off an edge, glue it on a card and make a list of your fabrics, otherwise it is quite easy to forget what you have.

Plastic drawstring bags have the merit of being transparent enough to see through and will squash into a small space, but the fabric can get rather creased and musty. Such bags can be hung on hooks behind a door.

# COLOURING AND PRINTING FABRICS

Modern techniques for dyeing and printing on a small scale are very easy and straightforward. Many people buy only plain fabrics and colour these with paints and dyes because, in spite of the enormous variety of available fabrics, just the right colour can be elusive. Subtle colours and particular patterns can be difficult to find, but by dyeing, painting and printing, it is easy to produce some lovely shades, and unique and interesting patterns.

Printing can be done on fabric which has been dyed first for background colour.

The aim should be to colour and print pieces which can then be cut up into appropriate shapes and used to create a patchwork or an appliqué.

**Always make sure that fabrics which have to be washed are absolutely colour fast.** Artefacts can be dry-cleaned if necessary.

## A. DYES

Dyeing is a scientific process therefore materials should be measured accurately to get the best results. Domestic hot and cold water dyes are available from haberdashery departments in large stores, craft suppliers and ironmongers.

*Dyed, marked and tie-dyed fabrics used for patchwork.*

Hot water dye is suitable for all natural and synthetic fabrics except acrylic.

Cold water dye is suitable only for natural fabrics and viscose.

Fabrics can be tinted by removing from the dye-bath after only a few minutes.

Full directions are always printed on the container.

When dyeing fabric, keep a small piece of the original to compare with the result. Keep a note of the type of fabric and the length of time it remains in the dye-bath. This information will be useful if you want to dye a larger amount at a later date and need to repeat the colour.

Preparation for dyeing all fabrics is the same.

    a.   Protect yourself and all surfaces with newspaper or plastic sheet;

    b.   Squeeze the fabrics in hot water and liquid detergent to remove dressing, and rinse.

**1.  Hot water dyeing**  (One small tin plus one tablespoon of salt will dye 200-250 grams dry fabric.)

Dissolve the dye powder in 0.5 litres of boiling water. Add the salt.

Use a large rustproof pan filled with enough water to cover the fabrics. Add the dye solution, stir well and put in the wet fabrics.

Bring to the boil and simmer gently for approximately 20 mins, less if you want a paler colour.

**2.  Cold water dyeing**  (One small tin plus four tablespoons of salt and one tablespoon of washing soda will dye 200-250 grams of dry fabric.)

Dissolve the dye powder in 0.5 litres warm water. Dissolve salt and washing soda in hot water.

Fill a rustproof basin (e.g. plastic) with enough water to cover the fabrics and add the dye solution. Stir thoroughly.

Put in the wet fabrics and stir constantly for a few minutes. Keep the fabrics submerged. Leave for approximately one hour, stirring gently now and again.

In both methods take out the dyed pieces and rinse until the water runs clean.

Squeeze the dyed fabrics in very hot water and liquid detergent to remove any loose dye.

If you want to dye a large amount of fabric, this can be done safely and successfully in any washing-machine — including automatics. Use dye which is specifically manufactured for the purpose.

Large quantities of small pieces of fabric should be loosely tied in a muslin bag.

Dye residue is completely removed from the washing-machine by running a hot programme with a cup of detergent and another of bleach.

Dye patterned and medium-dark fabrics as well as pale colours to see the effect of over-dyeing.

**3.  Random dyeing**  (see page 32)

**4.  Resist dyeing with cold water dye**  (Tie-dye) Fabrics can be bunched and tied tightly round with pieces of cotton or string, so that the dye cannot penetrate the parts of the fabric underneath the ties. When the fabric is dyed and rinsed, and the ties removed, the undyed parts of the fabric will form a pattern.

The ties form a resist to the dye. Different ties make different patterns.

More regular patterns can be made by arranging the fabric in folds, pleats and gathers before tying and dyeing.

Ironing the folds makes a more definite pattern.

Try the effect of rubber bands or knots rather than string.

Use the longest stitch on a machine to make lines of machine stitching.

Gather tightly.

Keep the bundles submerged during the dyeing process

After an hour, remove the tied fabrics, untie knots, etc. and rinse the fabric as above.

*Tie-dye cotton. Criss-cross pattern made by vertical machining with satin stitch and horizontal machining and gathering. Stitches removed after dyeing. Circles made by circular gathering and wrapping with crochet yarn.*

**5. Resist dyeing in a microwave oven.** Fabrics can also be dyed successfully in a microwave oven, using a specialist dye and carefully following the manufacturer's instructions.

The fabric has to be bunched up to fit into a small basin so the uneven dyeing forms patterns.

Fabrics can also be folded and tied to make tie-dye patterns.

Be particularly careful when removing the bowl of dye liquid from the microwave as this can be extremely hot.

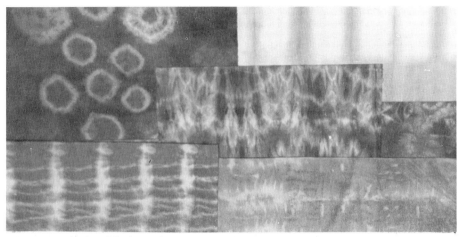

*Microwave dyeing. Variety of patterns made by folding, wrapping with rubber bands, pleating, crumpling.*

## B   FABRIC PAINTS AND CRAYONS

There are two distinct types of fabric paint and crayons.
    a.   Direct crayons and paints can be used on ANY fabric.
    b.   Transfer paints and crayons can only be used on synthetic fabrics. Although they will print on mixed fibres, the colours are not so permanent and are apt to fade.
    All fabric paints and crayons are made fast by ironing.

Very simple methods of patterning are most effective like line patterns and criss-cross patterns already mentioned (see p.15). The fabrics created can then be used for patchwork and appliqué.

### DIRECT PAINTS AND CRAYONS

**1   Direct pastel crayons** (Pentel)   These crayons make smudgy patterns like pastels.
    Any type of pale-coloured fabric can be used and should be pinned onto a piece of softboard covered with a pad of newspaper.
    a.   Make patterns and textures by scribbling and doodling in lines. The colours can be mixed directly on the fabric.
    b.   Take rubbings of hard raised textured materials like canvas.

**2.   Direct fabric markers**   Fabric markers are available in bright, clear colours and make definite lines. Both thick and thin markers are available. and some markers can be refilled.
    a.   Make definite patterns, vertical and horizontal lines and criss-cross patterns. Fill in some areas.
    b.   Use the markers with other fabric paints and crayons to give more definite patterns and sharp edges.

**3.** **Direct paints** These come in a number of forms: transparent paint suitable for pale coloured fabric, and opaque and metallic paints for dark colours. Most paints are water soluble, but check this in the instructions.

Work on a softboard covered with newspaper and kitchen paper to make a padded surface. Pin the fabric over this.

a. Texture by sponging or dabbing onto wet or dry fabric. Different materials give different results. Try sponge, screwed up paper, a stiff paintbrush etc.

b. Stencils can be used to make a more definite pattern. These can be made from stencil paper (manilla paper treated with linseed oil). Cut the stencil with a craft knife. Pin the fabric onto softboard. Pin or stick the stencil in place with Spray Mount adhesive. Sticky-backed plastic or masking tape are alternatives.

Dab or spray through the stencil. Use a diffuser or a perfume or plant spray. Alternatively splattering the surface with an old toothbrush gives a good texture, particularly if you use two colours. Car spray paints are effective, but it is important to follow the instructions on the container and use in a well ventilated room. Blow a thin layer of paint, allow to dry and repeat.

Allow to dry before removing the stencil.

Protect the floor and surrounding area with newspaper.

*French Landscape. Machine appliqué. Fabric shapes decorated with machine pattern and fabric print.* (see p.86)

c. Print with small handmade blocks. Vegetables such as potatoes or carrots are easy to use and make very effective patterns.

Using a craft knife, cut across the vegetable to form a flat surface. Cut or gouge a pattern. Cut away material from the edge of the pattern.

Pour fabric paint onto a thin layer of sponge in a saucer. Dab the printing block onto this and press onto the fabric. This gives a good even print.

Stick Prints: small patterned objects like buttons can be stuck to the end of a piece of wooden dowelling rod. Use a suitable waterproof glue, e.g. Araldite. Allow to dry completely before using.

Other small objects can be utilised as printing blocks, corks, india-rubbers, string stuck on a wood block, pieces of card, etc.

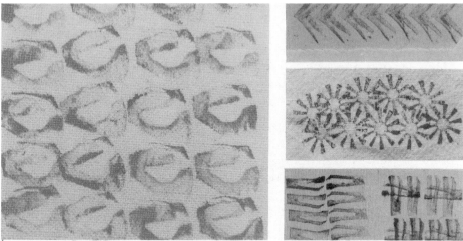

*Variety of block patterns made with potato prints, button prints, strips of india rubber.*

**4. Silk paint with wax resist** These paints are fluid enough to run through fine fibres, so just a drip will spread over a wide area.

a.  Colour can be dripped or painted on wet or dry fabric.

b.  Coarse salt scattered on the painted surface will make patterns as the pigment is drawn to the salt crystals.

c.  To stop the colours running together the paint can be isolated in particular areas by using a resist. A special gutta is sold with the silk paints, but this method can also be used very successfully with hot batik wax and a brush or a tjanting. A thermostatically controlled wax pot is available or wax can be melted in a tin, heated in a pan of hot water.

Hold the fabric taut in an embroidery ring or pin onto a frame.

Paint or trail the resist (gutta or wax) onto the silk to form isolated areas and islands. Make sure the resist has penetrated the fabric completely. it should go right through to the back. Allow to dry.

Drip different coloured paints into the isolated areas.

Allow to dry.

Iron the fabric between two pieces of blotting paper or newsprint to absorb the wax, and make the colour fast.

Wash in hot water and detergent or have the fabric dry-cleaned.

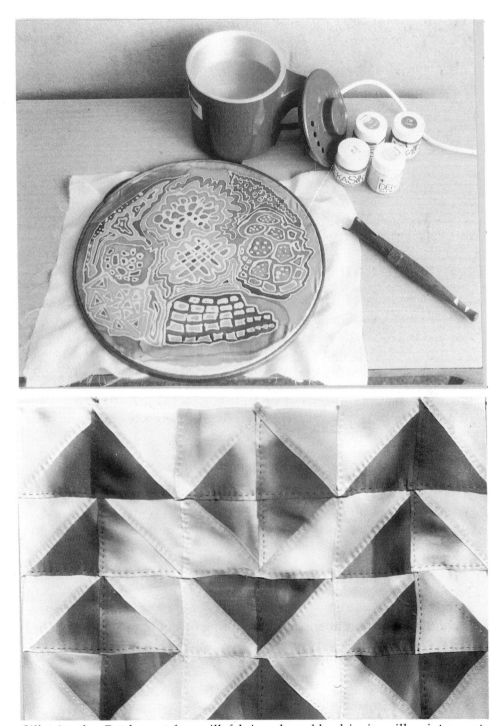

*Silk triangles. Patches cut from silk fabric, coloured by dripping silk paint on wet fabric, so that pale tints merge into dark tones. Hand sewn with silk thread with stitches on the surface.*

## TRANSFER PAINTS AND CRAYONS

These paints or crayons are drawn or painted on paper, then ironed onto synthetic fabric. Use thin non-absorbent paper for paints, and greaseproof paper for crayons.

**1.  Transfer crayons**
   a.  Make lines and all-over patterns, then cut these up and reassemble.
   b.  Use the crayons for taking rubbings from materials like corrugated card, patterned glass and texture on materials like fabric, wood, etc.

**2.  Transfer paints**
   **a.**  Use the paints to make texture on paper by sponging, printing and spraying.
   b.  Some types of paint are thick enough to drag with a comb or the edge of a piece of card. (see opposite)

## PRINTING METHOD WITH TRANSFER COLOURS

Protect the ironing-board with a piece of newspaper and kitchen paper. Lay the fabric on the board and place the patterned paper face down on it. Press, so the pattern does not smudge. The iron should be hot enough to make a clear, bright print.

Because the colours are apt to change when they are ironed onto fabric, begin by making a list of all the colours on a spare piece of synthetic fabric, and keep the results for reference.

The papers can be printed as they are, but far better to cut or tear them and reassemble them in patterns.

   1.  Cut simple shapes squares, circles etc,
Arrange in patterns face down on the fabric, cover with another patterned paper and iron.

   If the cut-outs are small, they can be stuck on another piece of paper first.

   2.  Torn shapes give a different effect, so try these too.

   3.  Cut out simple flower, leaf or house shapes as well as geometric shapes.

   4.  Most paints will give several prints. Crayons usually only give two.
Make use of the fact that the second and subsequent prints will be paler.
Keep all the unironed bits of paper which can be used later.

Some of these techniques for dyeing and printing are mentioned more specifically throughout the text in experiments with colour, pattern and shape.

All the paints and colours can be used together if necessary, as long as the background fabric is suitable. Iron and fix one type of colour before adding another.

Keep in mind the fact that the printed fabrics created might be used for patchwork shapes or for appliqué. They will also be used alongside other printed and plain fabrics. Because of this it is a good idea to keep all the fabrics you have printed. Even those which do not appear very successful at first sight, might be just what is needed later on, in a particular context.

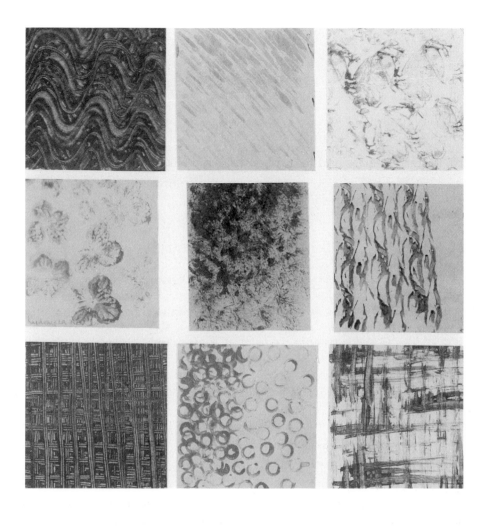

*Hexagons. Synthethic fabric coloured with transfer paints.*

# COLOUR AND FABRIC

Colour is an integral part of the final design. The juxtaposition of coloured fabrics and the reaction of the surrounding fabric colours to one another and to the background fabric is of the greatest importance.

Pieces can actually be spoilt because areas of colour are unbalanced. Some colours are very strong, bright and dominant, while others appear to recede into the background.

Some colours have a warm feel, while others are chilly.

A small proportion of one colour seems to give a lift to adjacent colours where a larger area of the same colour can deaden.

Look at your own collection of fabrics and divide them into groups of colour which look good together. Patchwork and appliqué are crafts which make use of pieces of coloured fabric grouped together. Each piece has to fit in, not only with the adjacent piece, but also to add to the overall effect.

Instead of using paints and crayons to provide the colour in a design, use small pieces of fabric or coloured paper. This makes it much easier to see how some of these experiments might eventually be used for a design for a larger piece of work.

Keep all work in a file for reference.

*Le Mont St. Michel. Appliqué with shiny and transparent fabrics. Machine embroidery.*

# THE COLOUR WHEEL

Some people manage to organise colour schemes by instinct, and produce lovely subtle pieces which would be very complicated to analyse, while others use schemes which are discordant, but exciting and unique. It would be a pity if everything was standardised to such an extent that it was boring and predictable. So if you want to use particular colours, you should.

Not everyone has the confidence to do this, however, so many people use a colour wheel to help them organise satisfactory colour schemes.

Colour wheels are used by many art and craft practitioners in all fields.

The colours of the spectrum are arranged in order in a circle. Certain combinations of colour work well together.

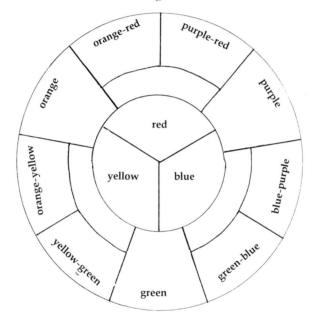

*The colour wheel*

# HUES

Some colours are bright and clear, neither dark nor pale. These are called hues.

There are three primary colours — red, blue, yellow.

Three secondary colours, which are the primary colours mixed in equal proportions, so:

    red and yellow make orange,
    yellow and blue make green,
    blue and red make purple.

Tertiary colours — These are a mixture of one primary colour and the secondary colour adjacent — yellow and orange make yellow-orange etc.

### Experimenting with hues

The way secondary and tertiary colours are created can be seen in practice in:

**1.  Random dyeing or space dyeing.** using cold water dyes. (See page 22).

This is an excellent method of seeing primary colours actually mixing together to make secondary colours. Fabrics can be given exciting rainbow or tonal effects by using red, yellow and blue dye.

To enable the dyes to run together without mixing too much, only a small amount of salt and soda solution is used.

Mix the salt and soda solutions first. They will keep indefinitely in screw-topped bottles which should be labelled.

Salt solution: 250 grams salt to 1 litre water
Soda solution: 200 grams soda to 1 litre water.

YOU WILL NEED

*A wide but shallow plastic container (e.g. cat litter tray or a washing-up bowl).*
*Strips of pale, natural fabric (e.g cotton or silk)*
*Dyes in the three primary colours*

WHAT TO DO

a.   Prepare the fabrics and arrange round the edge of the tray. Wet or dry fabrics can be used. Dry fabrics take on a more definite colour.
b.   In a jam jar, mix one flat 5ml teaspoon of dye powder with a little hot water to dissolve. Add one tablespoon salt solution and two tablespoons soda solution. Add cold water to give approx half a jam jar of colour.
c.   Mix the different colours in separate jars.
d.   Spoon the dyes over the fabrics, taking care the dye goes through the fabrics but does not swamp the tray. It is a good idea to have some areas of one colour, then some areas where the colours can mix — yellow with blue, blue with red etc.
e.   Leave for half an hour or more. Do not stir.
f.   Rinse until the water runs clean.
g.   Squeeze in hot water and liquid detergent.

Notice how the fabric has taken the dye in patches, where colours have mixed.

Go on to try other colour mixes.

### 2  Using melted transfer crayons
YOU WILL NEED
*Fabric transfer crayons*
*100% polyester fabric*
*Greaseproof paper (approx 20 x 10cm)*

WHAT TO DO

a.   Sharpen some of the yellow and red crayons catching the flakes on one half of the paper.

b.   Fold the other half over and iron. Open immediately and allow the crayon to harden.

c.   Cut the paper into squares or triangles. Arrange on the fabric and then iron. You can try this with various combinations of colour to see what happens when colours mix. Some of the results will be more successful than others.

*Melted transfer crayon printed on synthetic satin. Clamshell patches bonded to cotton background with bondaweb, to be attached with machine satin stitch.*

## 3   Weaving

YOU WILL NEED

*Several strips of paper, fabric or ribbon in both blue and red*
*Softboard and pins.*

WHAT TO DO:

a.   Pin out the blue strips in horizontal lines.

b.   Weave the red strips from top to bottom.

   Look at the result from a distance. What colour is created?

   Go on to weave other colours together. Notice how this creates a design which might be used for patchwork.

## TONES

Fabrics of a similar colour can differ because they are heavily textured or patterned. A piece of red silk can never look exactly the same as a scrap of red wool.

Some materials are dark and matt, some are pale and shiny and so on. Patterned fabrics also have a predominant colour and tone.

Look at a group of coloured fabrics through half closed eyes and you will see that some register dark, and some light.

The dark TONES are called SHADES
The light TONES are called TINTS.

The tone of the colour used is particularly important in both patchwork and appliqué. Dark tones should balance light and medium tones.

For the following experiments, cut out freehand and use commercial and hand-printed or dyed fabrics or paper.

1.  Cut a strip from each fabric in one colour group. Arrange from the darkest through to the lightest. Glue down.

2.  Cut two or three squares from each piece and arrange in light and dark chequer-board pattern.

3.  Think of different ways of arranging similar squares, e.g. all the pale squares in the middle with the dark squares round the edge and so on.

4.  Choose a range of larger pieces of fabric in ANY colour from dark to light, and dye these in a HUE like green, retaining a small piece of each fabric for comparison.

This is a good way of using up pieces of fabric which you do not like very much and produces a range of fabrics in tones of the ONE colour.

5.  Compare a coloured pattern printed on white with a plain fabric in the same colour. Notice how the white lightens the colour.

Look for the reverse: the same colour printed on a dark (or black) background. Notice how the colour is darkened.

Use squares of these fabrics together to make patterns.

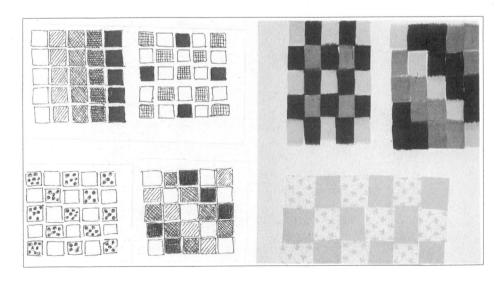

6.   Look at your collection of patterned fabric to see if any is printed with light and dark tones of one colour. Find a plain fabric to match the light tone and a plain fabric to match the dark tone.

Cut several squares from each. Arrange in a pattern.

7.   Take a plain, bright coloured fabric. Cut in half and print spots or stripes or a very simple motif all over one half using a dark shade of the same colour or black.

Print in a paler colour or white on the other half.

Continue arranging various combinations of cut-out squares within a colour group. Stick down those you like.

Notice how printing either darkens or lightens fabrics and how tones of one colour look tranquil or harmonious together.

Working with the tones of one colour makes it obvious just how important tone is in pattern making and how each shape affects all the others in the pattern.

## ANALAGOUS COLOURS

These colours are adjacent to each other on the colour wheel.

They look pleasing together because they contain a proportion of each other.

For example:

> blue, blue-red, red-blue and red.
> green, green-blue, blue.

Look at combinations of analagous colours around a colour wheel.

*Machine patchwork with triangles using striped fabric*

1.   Find some analagous coloured fabrics in different tones in translucent fabric like chiffon, organza, etc.
   Cut the fabrics into different sized circles and arrange on a background fabric with some of the shapes overlapping.
   Notice how the background colour affects the colour of the fabric circles, and how the colours are affected at the overlap.
2.   Weave strips of analagous colours together on softboard.
3.   Look through your patterned fabric and see if any of these are printed with analagous colours.
   Match plain colours with these.
   There are a large number of what appear to be indeterminate colours like grey, brown and olive which do not fit neatly into these schemes.
1.   Using water based paints, mix hues together in different proportions. Mix some of the resulting secondary and tertiary colours with small, medium and large proportions of black or white or grey (black plus white).
   As you mix, paint the individual colour mixes onto squares of white paper (dressmakers graph paper) and try and note which colours you have used. It is possible to create an infinite number of different and surprising colours. Match these with fabrics.
2.   Look at the samples of paint in the paint mixer in a large department or a DIY store and notice the gradations of colour mixes.
   Look again at the fabrics which are mixtures of many colours and put them into their nearest colour category.

## COMPLEMENTARY COLOURS

   Complementary colours are contrasts. These colours are opposite in the colour wheel and show each other up to good advantage provided the proportions are correct.
   A little orange shows up blue, even if the orange is a very dark shade and the blue a very pale tint.
   Similarly, red and green are complementary and so are purple and yellow.
   It only takes a dash of complementary colour to give a lift to a group of analagous colours. This can be seen in many of the paintings of Vincent Van Gogh, where dashes of brilliant, dark ultramarine blue are painted against yellows and pale golds, while red and terracotta roofs appear in green fields and hills. The final effect can be exciting or disturbing, but never dull or restful.
   On the other hand, equal proportions of complementary colour can cancel each other out to such an extent that a grey effect is produced.

## COLOUR SCHEMES

Tone and colour, pattern and texture give each fabric its own character and individuality. Some fabrics go together beautifully while some detract.
However good the technique, the whole can be completely spoiled by unbalanced colour and tone.

*Oak Leaves Appliqué Quilt. 19th Century American.*

Colour is used by designers to make things look attractive to encourage us to buy. It is used extensively in advertising in catalogues, shop windows and on television, and we can analyse and make use of attractive colour schemes where they happen to fit in with what we are doing.

If bright or garish colours are not suitable, perhaps the tints or shades of those particular colours could be used instead.

Notice what proportion of each colour has been used and the proportion and contrast of light and dark tone.

These theories can be useful when colouring and printing pieces of fabric and when designing for patchwork and appliqué.

## MAKING A COLLAGE

Collage means to stick. Cut-out pieces of fabric and paper are simply stuck down onto a background to see the effect the colours create.

If you are designing an appliqué picture or a patchwork, making a collage of cut and torn pieces gives a good idea of how the final piece will actually look, and an opportunity to alter the tone and colour at an early stage if necessary.

A collage can be made on a small scale, but since scale is important and a larger finished piece might look different, eventually it will be worth doing a section of design to size, to see how the combination of colours appears.

Fabric collage has a particularly attractive and unique look all its own

## MATERIALS FOR COLLAGE

Background for collage can be paper or fabric. This should be stiff so that the pieces will not slide off. Fabric can be stiffened by pasting it to paper, card, polystyrene, board, etc.

If you use PVA glue, this glue can be spread evenly on a lining paper, then the background fabric can be smoothed on. Iron so that the materials bond together.

Glueing fabric to a rigid surface like card or hardboard often distorts it. Glue another piece of fabric or paper onto the back to compensate for this. Paper-backed hessian is a useful background and can be pasted to a piece of cardboard with wallpaper paste.

Any colour photograph can be turned into a useful design.

YOU WILL NEED
*A colour photograph or a reproduction of a painting*
*Fabrics, coloured paper*
*Glue, ruler and pencil*
*Background paper or fabric*
*Graph paper*

WHAT TO DO
1.  Divide the whole picture into squares with a narrow ruler.
2.  Draw out a similar area of squares on cartridge paper or use graph paper.

3. Look at each individual square in the picture and decide which is the predominant colour. Cut a square of fabric matching as near as possible in tone and colour and affix to the appropriate square on the paper. Cut free-hand because it does not matter if the squares overlap slightly.

This picture could be used as the design of a patchwork, or it could be machined and made into an appliqué.

This exercise can also be carried out using graph tracing paper.

*Squared tracing paper placed over photograph. Colour dotted in.*

## COLOUR PHOTOCOPIES

Some modern colour photocopiers have a facility which will turn a colour photograph into a mosaic of coloured squares. This is an extremely easy and useful way of producing a design from a photograph.

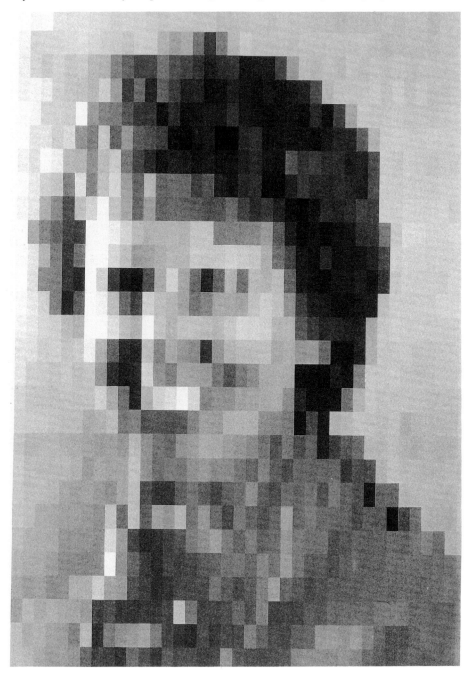

# PATCHWORK WITH FABRIC STRIPS

## LINES AND STRIPES

Fabrics can be put together in many different ways to produce areas of geometric or representational pattern or pictures.

One of the easiest and most effective methods of design is simply to use strips of fabric cut, rearranged and sewn together to create patterns. These methods of piecing together strips of fabric give rise to several forms of patchwork which are well known and traditional. The techniques themselves are all easy, it is the choice of colour, pattern and tone which gives the effect.

### Preparing The Fabric

Fine but strong woven fabrics can sometimes be torn rather than cut and this can be quicker and easier. Fabrics like cotton, organza, organdie, and some silks will tear from selvage to selvage. Start with a cut into the edge.

Some fabrics are spoilt along the edge by tearing, so test a piece first. If you are using printed fabric make sure that the fabric tears evenly across the pattern. If it does not, make an accurate template or pattern with card and a ruler, using a set square to construct a true right angle. Evenweave fabrics can be cut along the grain of the fabric.

To remove the puckers, iron along the edge of the fabric, holding the iron down firmly and pulling the fabric under it. Alternatively, pull the fabric over the edge of a table.

The different combinations of fabric colours, tones and patterns, and the arrangement of a variety of widths of fabric give an almost infinite number of possibilities.

## A)   STRIP PATCHWORK

Strips of fabrics are sewn together to make an area of striped fabric.
WHAT TO DO
1.   Cut or tear strips so that when they are joined, a block of striped fabric approx 20cm square is made. Shorter strips should be joined first if necessary.
2.   Pin the pieces with right sides together and machine or sew by hand with running stitch. Use the machine foot to gauge the seam allowance. Press the seams open.

Try some of the following combinations of fabric, working on a small scale.

a.   Plain cotton fabrics in tones of one colour, or light and dark tones of analagous colour or a colour combination you like. You might print with a small block pattern along a fabric strip.

b.   Patterned fabrics with plain fabrics which pick up one or two of the colours in the pattern.

c.   Silks, satin and exotic fabrics. The resulting fabric can be further decorated with lines of machine stitching in silk or metallic thread. Remember that ribbons and lace are also strips of fabric and use these too.

d.   Woven tweed fabrics in subtle colours often go together.

e.   A range of all kinds of plain and patterned fabrics in the same weight which have been dyed together.

f.   Velvet and corduroy.

Pin the fabrics in order on a piece of softboard and look at them from a distance to make sure you have created the impression you want.

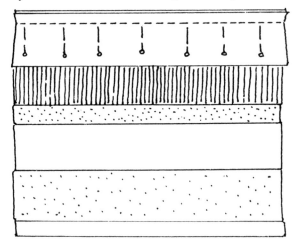

*Joining Strips.*
*Pin, tack, stitch*
*with right side*
*facing.*
*Seam allowance:*
*6mm*

**B) SEMINOLE PATCHWORK**   This technique is used by the Seminole Indians in Florida, North America and is based on their traditional patterns.

Strips of bright coloured cotton are joined to make a fabric which is cut again and rejoined. Sometimes the cut strips are angled so the fabric is on the cross. All the sewing is done on a sewing machine.

The intricate bands of pattern formed are built up to make a fabric. Although the patterns appear complicated, they are much easier to achieve than would appear at first sight.

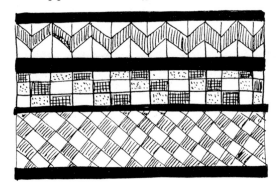

**Planning the design:** Seminole patchwork can be planned first with coloured or patterned paper.

Try out the technique on a small scale.

YOU WILL NEED

*Striped paper 30 x 9cm. (This can be made by sticking strips of paper onto a background or use thick felt pens or highlighters, or commercial striped wrapping paper.)*

WHAT TO DO

Use the width of a ruler to cut strips at right angles to the stripes. Arrange these in different ways.

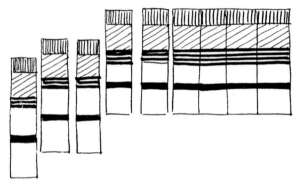

1.   Turn every alternate strip upside down.
2.   Turn the strips on their side to make a chequered stripe. Place one stripe under the other so the colours are staggered.

More and different patterns can be created by:
1.   making the stripes in different widths.
2.   cutting across the stripes in different widths
3.   cutting at angle 90° or 45°
4.   turning the pieces either alternately upside down or on their side.

The Seminole patterns are precise and accurate, but more irregular patterns can be made by cutting lines at different angles and rearranging.

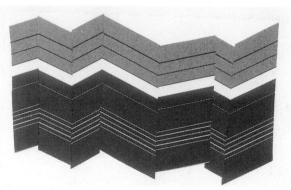

*Seminole design with wrapping paper*

**Using fabrics:** The Seminole Indians used brightly coloured cotton fabric to make their linear patterns, using plain coloured and black strips to separate and show up the patterned borders.

*METHOD*
1. Plain coloured cotton is an easy fabric to use. Choose three tones of one colour; light, medium and dark.
2. Cut three strips but in different widths.
3. Pin with right sides together and sew on a sewing-machine, using the foot as a seam allowance. Press.
4. Cut pieces from this fabric, measuring carefully to make sure the angles are accurate.
5. Pin with right sides together and machine. Press.

Fabrics used can be as many and varied as those combinations mentioned above for making strip patchwork, so experiment.

All the fabric in one piece of work should be similar in weight and fibre, but a flimsy fabric which is just right can be bonded to cotton or backed with iron on interfacing.

*'Beginning to See the Light' by Alison Harding. Log cabin wall hanging.*
*Notice the arrangement of the blocks, creating an all-over tonal pattern.*

## C ) LOG-CABIN PATCHWORK

This is another traditional method of using strips of fabric. The name is
Canadian, but the same technique has been used in all parts of the world
for hundreds of years, but called by different names. Ribbons can be used
instead of fabric strips.

Again the tones of the fabrics and how they are arranged are of the
greatest importance. These patterns can look stunning when seen from a

45

distance and are often used for large areas of fabric such as bedcoverings.

Traditionally, the strips are sewn round a central square of fabric, one at a time to make a square block.

The technique can be done by hand or with a machine, and any fabric can be used, depending on the function of what is being made.

The fabrics should be of a similar weight.

*Method of making a log cabin block:* try the technique with cotton fabrics.

*One block of log cabin. Detail of bedcover. Poppy design using transfer paint. Roberta Warren.*

## YOU WILL NEED
*Light and dark tone cotton fabrics.*

## WHAT TO DO
1.  Cut or tear strips of dark toned fabric, and strips of pale toned fabric, each approx 6cm wide.
2.  Cut a square of fabric about 10 x 10cm.
3.  With right side together, pin and sew a pale strip along the top of the square. Use the width of the machine foot as a seam allowance. Cut off the superfluous end to make a rectangle.
4.  Pin and sew a pale strip along the adjacent side of the rectangle and trim.

5.   Keep sewing on strips in sequence: two light, then two dark, to form a block of fabric. Alternatively, the strips of fabric can be sewn in different sequences of light and dark to make different patterns, for example, four light then four dark, all light and all dark, etc.

There are no rules about the type of fabric used for experiment and for wall-hangings, although fabrics used should be the same type and weight. Printed and plain fabrics look entirely different from transparent and translucent fabrics or ribbons or all metallic fabrics.

Try out patterns with cut paper to see their effect and use unusual combinations of fabrics, including fabrics you have printed yourself.

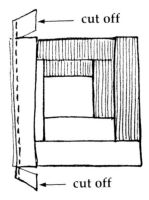

*Experiments with log cabin.  Mig Holder*

## PRINTING STRIPED FABRICS.

It is easy to print striped fabrics by hand, or to use commercial striped fabric as a basis for further fabric printing.
Methods:
1.   Use masking tape. Pin or tape a piece of well-washed plain coloured fabric, poplin or polyester cotton, to a piece of soft board over a wad of newspaper.
   If you are going to use the fabric for patchwork, make sure the tape is stuck along the straight grain of the fabric. Pull a thread across the fabric to make sure.
   Paint or dab between the lines of tape with fabric paint, using a sponge or even screwed up paper.
   Spraying is also very effective, particularly car sprays, but make sure you use them in a well ventilated room. Read the instructions to see how to prevent clogging.
   Leave to dry, then remove the tape.
2.   Use transfer paints and crayons for synthetic fabrics. Texture or pattern papers and iron over the masking tape.
3.   Draw or paint stripes on paper using transfer crayons or paints. You can use a pencil and ruler to draw the lines, as these will not print.
4.   Cover a piece of paper with textures, using transfer paint or crayon. Cut the paper into strips with a craft knife and print.
5.   You can add more thin, well defined stripes to any of the above with a fabric marker.

### Commercial fabrics

There are numerous commercial striped fabrics available for use both in dress and soft furnishings. Many of these have strips of pattern alternating with strips of plain colour and these can be cut up and rearranged. This is particularly useful for making home furnishings where smaller artefacts can be made to match in with curtains and covers.

## USING STRIPED FABRICS

Strips of all the striped fabrics described above can be cut and reassembled to make interesting patterns similar to Seminole patchwork or as strips in log cabin.

Methods:
1.   Cut a length of striped fabric into pieces, all the same width. Turn every alternate piece upside down. Cut two different widths.
2.   Cut a length into squares, rearrange.
3.   Cut a length into squares, then cut across the diagonal of each. Make patterns with these by re-arranging. The patterns will be different if you cut across the other diagonal, or across both alternately. (see p.35)

4. Use a selection of strips for log cabin. Try cutting across as well as down the stripes.

Sometimes these patterns can be changed by incorporating other similar fabrics, or by using another part of the same fabric.

Measuring and cutting should be accurate, so that the stripes match exactly.

Sew the pieces together as before.

*Using striped fabric*

# PICTURES WITH STRIPES

## APPLIQUE PICTURES BASED ON STRIPES

It is surprising how often bands of colour, texture and pattern can be seen both in nature and in the man-made environment. Many flat or gently undulating landscapes can be simplified into coloured stripes.

Many seascapes almost look like a striped fabric, as the planes of colour recede and merge to the horizon.

Look also at photographs in magazines and notice that sections of background are often made up of bands of colour.

Colour schemes gleaned from observation of landscapes as well as photographs, can be made as a strip patchwork using commercial and hand-dyed fabrics.

Fabric can then be stretched on a frame and other fabric shapes or areas of stitchery can be applied. (see p.81)

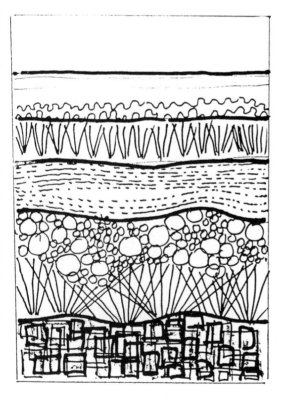 

51

Make a collection of photographs and diagrams of this sort of scene. The designs can be simplified and changed into lines of patterns and bands of colour and texture to make an abstract pattern.

*Flowers and Leaves. Printed leaves cut out and bonded to background. Transfer printed flowers on synthetic satin. Random dyed silk background.*

### Making a fabric mosaic
YOU WILL NEED:
*A photograph of a simple landscape*
*Tracing paper and glue*
*Scraps of coloured fabric to match the colours in the photograph*
*A firm background material.*

WHAT TO DO
1.   Make a tracing of the picture.
2.   Enlarge the tracing (see page 86) to the size you want. Trace and cut out the main areas. Place each in turn on the background, and outline with a fabric marker.
3.   Make a collage by sticking small pieces of coloured fabric in each area. Spread the glue thinly within each shape. Stick the pieces down,

overlapping to cover the background. You will find that two or three closely related colours of the same tone can be mixed together to give an impression of just one colour at a distance. Keep stepping back to see how the colours react.

4.   Leave to dry.

5.   The pieces can be sewn down with a machine, using free machine embroidery and machining in small spirals all over the mosaic or using one of the methods of hatching and cross hatching described on page 89.

Alternatively, each of these mosaics can be left as a collage without any stitching, and paper can be used as well as fabric to make a mixed media piece.

Using these simple line designs, continue to experiment.

Arrange and rearrange coloured fabric on a small scale, to see how the fabrics look together.

Make a habit of looking at the fabric groupings from a distance, with half-closed eyes to make sure you like the general effect.

It is surprising how dominant some quite small areas of colour can be and this can be altered at an early stage if necessary.

Have the self-confidence to use the colours and patterns you like. Above all, allow your own ideas to come out, trying to express what you feel and want to show.

*Fabric mosaic. Each area filled with small rectangles of tones of one colour.*

# PATCHWORK WITH GEOMETRIC SHAPES

Geometric shape is one of the elements of patchwork. Geometric fabric shapes are sewn together to form a fabric and only shapes which will interlock to form a flat area can be used.

The pattern is formed by the colour tones of the fabrics.

Only some regular geometric shapes (regular shapes have all sides of equal length) will interlock with one another to form a flat network without gaps.

These are triangles, squares and hexagons.

These regular shapes can be divided, i.e. a square can be bisected diagonally to form two triangles, *or* multiplied, i.e. each strip of fabric used for Seminole and Log-Cabin patchwork is actually a very long rectangle of uniform width (or a chain of squares) and these are subdivided into squares and triangles which were arranged and turned at various angles to create more patterns.

Semi-regular geometric shapes need a further shape to make an all over tesselation. Templates for these must either be carefully constructed or a commercial template should be used.

*Methods and techniques*
**TEMPLATES.** Accurate templates are required for paper and fabric patterns.

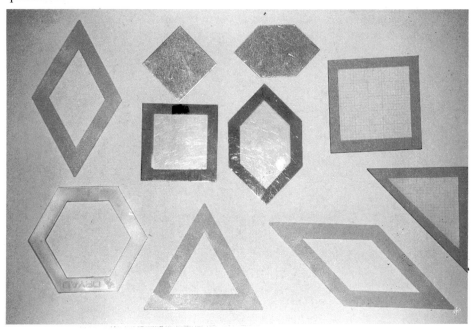

In former times, people relied on folding and cutting to make templates for patchwork. While this is still quite satisfactory provided it is done very carefully, we now employ commercial templates and use graph paper to make accurate shapes, because we have the technology to do so. Slight mistakes in a template are multiplied as the work progresses and although it is possible to rectify small inaccuracies, it is better and easier to work with templates which are true, right from the beginning.

Patchwork shapes need to be accurate so that the finished work lies flat.

**Commercial templates:**  These are machined from plastic or metal. Various types are available in all the useful geometric shapes.

a.   A metal template for cutting paper patterns and a larger plastic template. This is for cutting the fabric patch, and includes a seam allowance and a window, which makes it easy to see exactly which part of the fabric to use.

b.   A combination plastic template which includes the seam allowance and a cut out template shape.

The window or hole shows exactly which part of the fabric will be utilised.

*Patchwork using furnishing fabric.*

## Constructing templates.

1.  Templates can be made from graph paper stuck on card and/or coarse sandpaper which clings to the fabric to prevent the template slipping. A seam allowance should be included.
a.  Square graph paper or dressmakers graph paper is used for squares and right-angled triangles.
b.  Isometric graph paper is used for triangles, diamonds and hexagons.
2.  Templates can be constructed with a ruler, compasses and a protractor.

Affix the graph paper to the card or sandpaper and allow the glue to dry. Cut the template accurately with a steel rule and a craft knife.

Any seam allowances should be uniform throughout.
a.  A seam allowance of 6mm is suggested for hand sewing
b.  If you intend to use a machine, measure the distance between the edge of the presser foot and the needle. This enables you to use the presser foot as a guide.

## How to use templates:

**ENGLISH PATCHWORK:** This is the hand method using paper patterns which are covered with fabric. It is a traditional method of making patchwork and is very accurate.
1.  Use the metal template to cut paper patterns which will subsequently be covered with fabric.
2.  Use good quality stiff paper, like envelopes, writing paper, brown paper, greetings cards, etc.
3.  Place the paper on a softboard or a self-healing cutting board and cut round the template with a sharp craft knife.
*Note:* You need a paper pattern for every patch, so it is a good idea to cut quite a few at one time.

*Marking and cutting fabric patches (l) and paper patterns (r)*

*Fabrics:*    Choose all fabrics in the same fabric group; all silk, all cotton, etc.

Wash new fabric in case it shrinks and to test for dye fastness. *A piece of functional patchwork can be spoiled by one small patch which bleeds.* Always iron fabrics before beginning to work.

WHAT TO DO
1.    Place the larger window template on the straight grain of the fabric. With a small patterned or plain fabric, the shapes can be fitted together so as not to waste fabric.

With a large patterned fabric, exactly the right part can be chosen by looking through the hole or the window.
2.    Draw round the template with a hard pencil or a fabric marker. Felt-pen or a biro cause permanent marks.
3.    Cut out.
*Note:*    If you are cutting a large number of patches, these can be threaded on a piece of cotton to keep them together. Many people who have planned a large patchwork cut the patches as they collect suitable fabrics. Some manufacturers produce colour co-ordinated patches which can be utilised.
4.    Pin the paper pattern in the middle of the back of the fabric.
5.    Tack, folding the fabric neatly round the points and hold each point in place with a stitch. Press. Pin the pieces on soft board to see how they look.
6.    Place the patches right side together and oversew along the edge. Do not sew through the papers, which are removed with the tacking at the end of the project.

*English patchwork with diamonds. This pattern is called tumbling blocks. Microwave ' dyed fabrics and commercial print.*

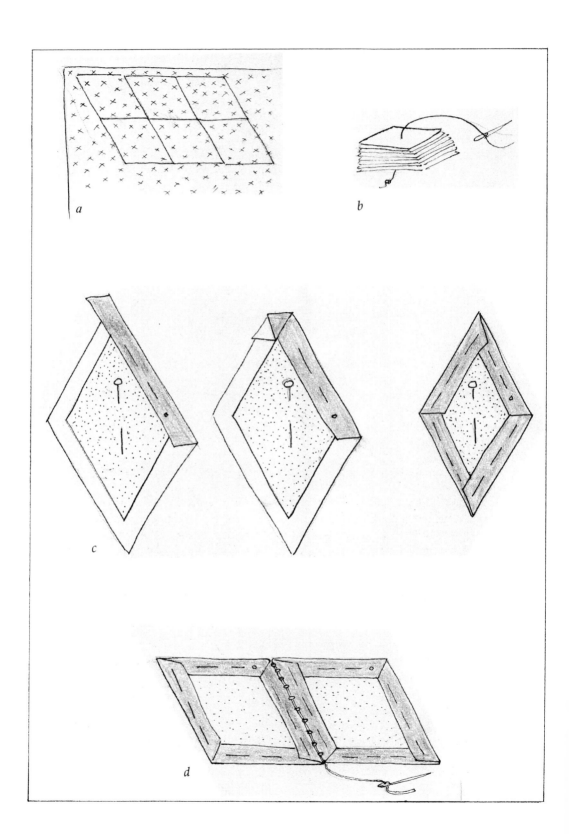

*The King. Free patchwork.*

The same method can also be used for any design which is made up of simple shapes without very acute angles.

Draw the design to the correct size on paper, or thin card for large shapes. Cut out and cover each paper pattern shape with fabric as above. Stitch and press.

Iron-on interfacing can be used instead of paper. This is permanent and gives a stiffer appearance and feel, but is very easy to use.

Mark out the interfacing as if it was paper and cut out. Iron onto fabric, leaving enough spare fabric round the edge for a seam allowance.

Fold and sew the fabric round the interfacing. Press and stitch.

Sheets of iron-on interfacing, printed with patchwork shapes and seam allowance already marked out are available.

**CLAMSHELL PATCHWORK** is constructed using a slightly different method.

WHAT TO DO
1. Pin the paper pattern to the FRONT of the fabric.
2. Fold the fabric to the back, creasing along the top curve of the pattern. Stitch without going through the paper pattern.
3. On the RIGHT side, mark the two curved sides with a fabric marker, but do not turn in.
4. Fix a horizontal plumb line between pins on softboard and pin a line of clamshells so the top curves just touch the line. Arrange the second line to the markings drawn on the patches.
5. Hem around the top curve of each shape.

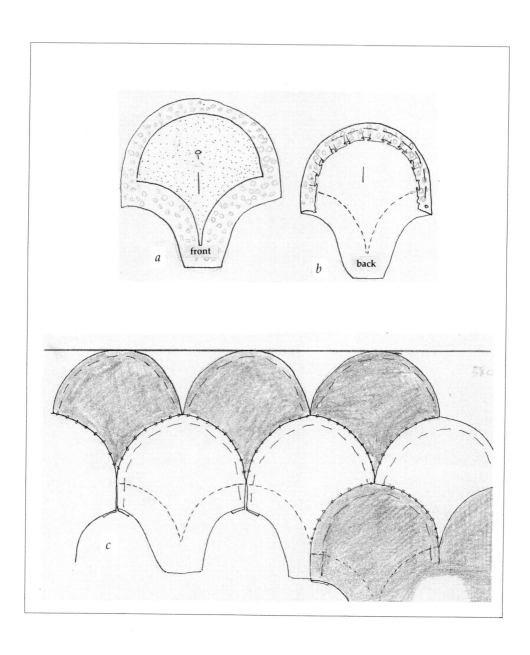

# AMERICAN PATCHWORK using graph paper templates.

WHAT TO DO
1.　Place the template on the wrong side of the fabric. Draw round inside and outside with a hard pencil. Cut out.
2.　Pin the patches right sides together. The pins should be placed at right angles to the seam line. Sew with a fine running stitch along the line of the seam allowance.
3.　Press, but do not open the seam.
4.　Assemble the patches in strips, then join the strips.

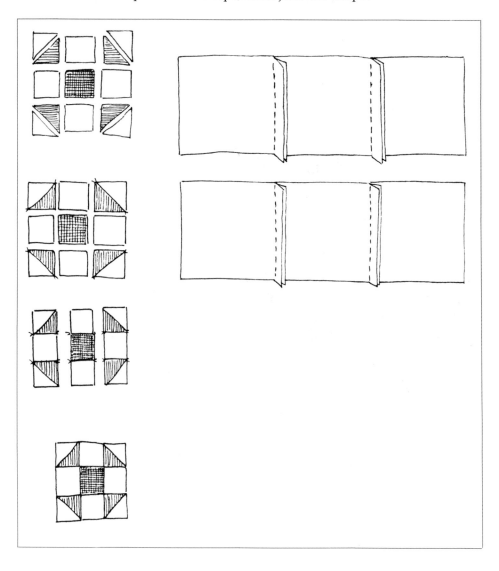

## SEWING-MACHINE METHOD

Many of the simple patchwork shapes like squares, triangles and diamonds can be sewn together with a machine. Cut patches with a seam allowance.

Again, the patches can easily be sewn together if they are first arranged, pinned and sewn in strips, and the strips machined together.

After machining, press the seams open, where possible.

Use the presser foot as a seam allowance gauge.

## APPLIQUE WITH PATCHWORK SHAPES

Some shapes like clamshells and hexagons cannot be machined satisfactorily, but they can be applied to a background fabric, and machined to that. (see p.33)

Cover the back of the fabric to be used with Bondaweb. Cut out the patchwork pieces to the exact size. Arrange on a piece of well ironed cotton or calico. Press.

Machine round each piece with straight stitch, then with a close zigzag. Instead of machine stitching, these shapes might be joined with hand embroidery using stitches like feather stitch or Cretan stitch.

### Crazy patchwork

In this method, irregular fabric shapes are arranged and sewn on to a background.

*Bag by Dawn Pavitt. Machine stitched crazy patchwork using men's silk ties and needlecord. Silk trimmings and hand embroidered decoration.*

WHAT TO DO
1.  Cut a piece of background fabric. Starting at one edge, arrange a few pieces on this and pin, or use Bondaweb as above. Sew down with decorative machine stitches, zigzag or hand embroidery stitches.
2.  Overlap with more patches and sew, continuing until the whole area is covered.

The choice of fabrics and the balance of the tones is important. Pin the pieces out first and look at them from a distance.

Try velvets and silks, all striped fabrics, all small patterned fabrics in similar tones and so on.

These simple skills create beautiful effects with all sorts of different fabrics. Do not let the techniques overshadow the joy of creating something unique.

*Victorian crazy patchwork. Velvets and silks decorated with embroidery stitches.*

# DESIGNING FOR PATCHWORK

A few fortunate people are able to create a sucessful patchwork without any initial planning. For most people, this is difficult, even impossible. However, even with no experience of drawing it is easy to work out designs for patchwork on paper. The design also makes it plain to see whether the patchwork will work successfully in fabrics.

Working on designs is an interesting activity in itself and many usable patterns can be created, some accidentally. Do not be satisfied with only one attempt at making patterns, but set some time aside to fill several pages with designs and ideas.

## GRAPH PAPER

This is easy to use because it is already marked out with a grid. If you have ideas about the sort of fabric you might eventually use, write this down alongside the design as you progress,

Using a black felt-tipped pen and a pencil and leaving some spaces blank will give tones of dark, medium and light.

Each geometric shape has a character of its own and each will produce different patterns. Concentrate on just one at a time, gradually exploring each shape in turn. For example:

**Hexagons** (using isometric graph paper)

a.  Arrange shapes to produce a cluster.
Repeat this cluster, either so that the shapes touch or are isolated.
Using two or three tones, fill in the shapes.
Reverse the tones so that you have a negative.

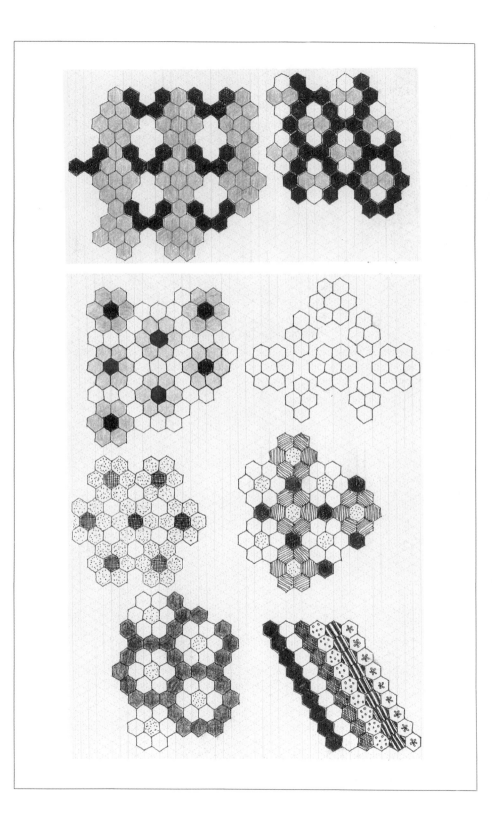

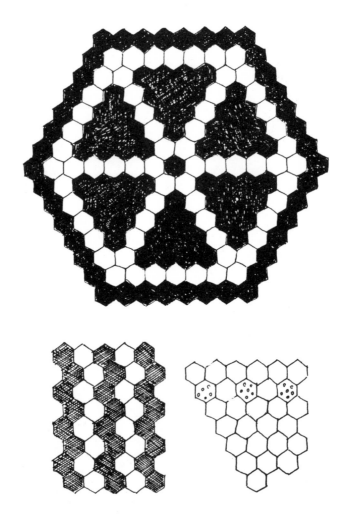

b.   Pack six hexagons round a central hexagon, then twelve round this cluster and so on. Use different tones to create patterns within this large cluster. Notice how the hexagons arranged in this way can be made to form a larger hexagon or a large diamond. This in turn repeats to form a pattern.

c.   Make line and border patterns using tone to create the pattern.

d.   Elongate the shapes to make irregular patterns.

As an interesting pattern is formed, isolate it and repeat it. Notice how pattern is formed within pattern. This can be used on a big or a small scale.

Go on to do the same experiments on isometric graph paper with *diamonds* and *triangles, squares, rectangles* and *triangles* on squared graph paper.

# DESIGNING FOR
# AMERICAN PATCHWORK

**Making a block pattern** (Use square graph paper).

This traditional form of pattern making was used in America by the early settlers in the last century. We are apt to think of them as cosy middle aged ladies, but in fact they were young women in their late teens and early twenties. Many had babies and children and had to live in the most inhospitable circumstances, before they were able to build their homes.

Fierce dust storms forced them to shelter in dug-outs for days at a time, while their husbands were away farming the land. They were desperately short of materials, and used every little bit of scrap fabric they could find. The beautiful abstract patterned coverings they produced were their only means of self expression.

The patterns were made in blocks which were then sewn together.

Each block of pattern was made by folding and cutting squares of paper for the templates, or just folding and cutting the fabric.

The design of each block was often based on blocks of four, nine or sixteen squares, and some of these were divided and subdivided to form the patterns. Each pattern had a name for example, Corn and Beans, Monkey Wrench and so on.

Work out some blocks on squared graph paper.

*Nine block pattern. By using different tones and turning blocks, the basic pattern can be changed.*

## Putting blocks together.

Similar blocks can be put together to make bigger blocks. Blocks can be arranged all the same way up, or every alternate block can be rotated.

Two different block patterns can be used alternately.

Single blocks or groups of blocks can be separated with a plain square or with strips of plain colour

A block can be made in any regular shape which will interlock.

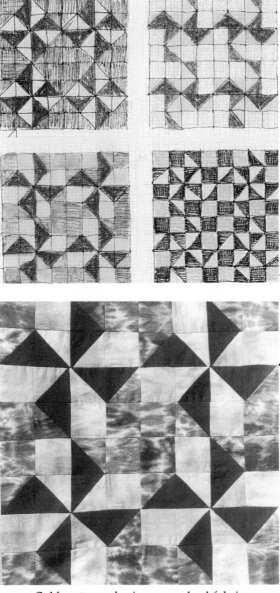

*Cold water and microwave dyed fabrics.*

69

## Other ideas

Instead of dividing the block into equal squares, it can be divided unequally, but systematically so that the pattern is distorted.

A block can be divided to make an interesting irregular pattern.

One single block can be used as the pattern for a large scale patchwork.

*Border patterns.*

70

## Amish quilts

The Amish people made beautiful dramatic quilts based on this idea. They used dark, clear coloured fabric to make up the patterns.

*Pavement at Fountains Abbey used as a basis for patterns.*

Working on tessellated designs in a variety of ways helps to understand how geometric shapes work and go together to form a myriad of patterns.

At the same time look around the environment for interlocking patterns. These can often be found in books and magazines and on other artefacts.

Tiles and paving stone patterns sometimes seen in old buildings are a rich source of ideas. Stained glass windows, particularly rose windows, have patterns which can be adapted to patchwork. It is sometimes possible to photograph a pattern on a floor or wall or buy a photograph of a window. These can be enlarged and photocopied, then coloured in and used as a basis for other designs.

## CHOOSING FABRICS

With experience it becomes easier to sort and match suitable groups of fabrics for a project. Keep the fabrics together as they are acquired.

A monochrome design might be worked exactly as it is in greys, blacks and whites or can be translated into coloured fabrics. These must be as near as possible IN TONE to the design, so that the pattern you have created is not spoilt.

*Same block pattern with different fabrics. Dyed, microwave dyed and commercial printed fabrics.*

Always be aware of the fact that a design can be carried out in different ways. Take any design and your collection of commercial and hand-printed fabric and try to imagine how it would look carried out in velvets or corduroys, printed cottons, wool tweeds or woven silks. Some fabrics, like dupion and shot silk, look different when seen from different angles because of the weave of the fabric, so the pieces can all be cut from the same fabric, but rotated to catch the light.

You can always choose just exactly the right part of a printed fabric with the window of the template.

Try to be aware of fabrics and how they look together. Do not be frightened of trying to produce a unique effect.

Choose a method of sewing which is most suitable.

*'The Path of the Lily Pond' by Roberta Warren. Patchwork quilt using printed floral cotton to represent flower borders and plain fabric for the paths and lavender edging The pond in the middle is made up of smaller squares.*

## FOLDED AND GATHERED PATCHWORK

Some methods use folded or gathered patches to create a more three-dimensional effect as well as giving some weight to the finished piece of work.

**Suffolk Puffs**   These are gathered circles, which are joined at the edges to make a textured overall pattern.

WHAT TO DO

1.   Make a template with compasses and card glued to sandpaper. The template should be approximately twice the size of the finished patch. (Try approx 15cm diameter)

2.   Cut circles and, with wrong side facing, turn in and gather each one round the edge. Use a strong thread and make sure it is secure. Finish off well.

3.   Oversew the puffs together. They can be joined in a regular grid pattern, or a variety of different sizes can be joined to make a texture.

Like all patchwork, the fabric used is of great importance to the finished appearance. Lightweight cotton is traditional, but translucent fabrics, plain calico, silk and metallic fabrics can all be used to great effect. Transparent puffs can be padded with bits of coloured fabric or wadding.

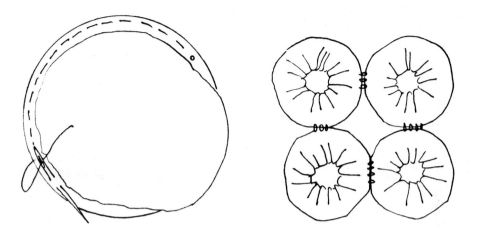

**Folded Patchwork**    Also called Folded Star or Somerset Patchwork.

WHAT TO DO

A square of fabric can be folded to make a right angled triangle.
Cut 5cm square of fabric and fold.

1.   Lines of these shapes will make an effective toothed border which can
be used round other patchwork patterns. Arrange the shapes along the
edge of a similar fabric with the right angle facing away from the edge. Pin,
machine and turn.

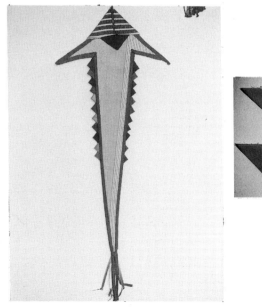

*Fishing Line (detail) by Alison Harding. Strip patchwork with folded patchwork trim.*

2. All-over pattern: the triangles can be applied to another square of fabric to make a textured surface.

Take a square of fabric and fold and mark the diagonals with a fabric marker or a hard pencil. Arrange the triangles with the right-angles to the centre.

Build up to make a pattern. As usual, the pattern can be changed by using various tones of colour and arrangement of shapes.

The pieces are sewn to the background along the edge, and caught down half way along each side.

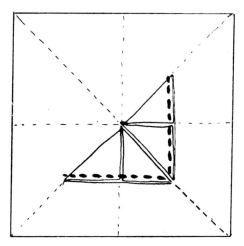

*Hold in position with one stitch at the centre. Stitch round.*

**Cathedral windows**    Small squares of contrasting colour are applied to
the seams between folded squares.

WHAT TO DO
1.   Cut a 15cm square of plain cotton fabric. Make a 5mm turn all round
and iron. Tack.
2.   Fold the corners into the centre and pin. Iron. Stitch the points in
position (right side).
3.   Oversew the squares together, right sides facing.
4.   Cut a square of contrasting fabric, very slightly smaller than the
diamond formed where the squares are seamed together. Pin.
5.   Pull each folded edge in turn over the contrasting fabric and hem
down, sewing through all the layers of fabric.

   This type of patchwork looks particularly effective when the squares are
in one colour only and the patches contrast. Experiment.

# APPLIQUE

An appliqué is made up of fabric shapes which are stitched to a background. These might be a series of geometric shapes arranged to make a pattern, or a collection of man-made or natural shapes which go together to form a picture.

### DESIGN FOR APPLIQUE

All designs start with an appealing idea. Often this will be quite vague; some pattern seen in the environment, a holiday photograph of a beautiful landscape, a sketch of a group of buildings or a lively newspaper cutting.

It might be just a fragment of pattern round a Christmas card or an interesting pattern of cut-out paper shapes. By making a habit of always noting down ideas in a sketch-book and collecting pictures and postcards which seem relevant, these ideas can be captured on paper. Then the initial idea can be turned into a working plan to produce a successful piece of work.

*Landscape inspired by primitive painting. Appliqué with hand stitching. Ruth Beesley*

## DESIGNING BASED ON GEOMETRIC PATTERN

Geometric shapes are as useful in appliqué as in patchwork and can be used as a rich source of design. Both linear and all-over pattern can be created. Design can be worked out easily with cut paper shapes.

WHAT TO DO

Choose just one geometric shape and work on this to make a number of different patterns.

Use coloured and printed paper and scraps of fabric, keeping to a particular colour scheme for each design.

Working freehand, cut a number of the pieces of the same shape in large, medium and small sizes, before beginning an arrangement.

Do not worry if the shapes are rather inaccurate as this often adds their appeal at the design stage.

Arrange some of the shapes on a background paper to see how they look:

1.  in a line;
2.  in a regular grid pattern, so the shapes either fit together or just touch;
3.  in a splattered pattern;
4.  within a large, similar shape.

Noticed how the pattern is changed:
1.  if shapes overlap;
2.  if different coloured papers are used;
3.  if different proportions of tone are used;
4.  if you cut the centre out of some of the shapes.

The same exercises can be carried out with different geometric shapes. Notice that some patterns look better if the shapes are all the same size, and others if shapes are cut in different sizes.

Choose fabrics to carry out some of these patterns in appliqué. Compare how patterns look when different types of fabric are used, for example silks and satins, transparent fabrics, wools, metallic fabrics, etc.

### Folding and cutting

Take a square of paper and fold in half, then half again. Cut into the folded edges and create a lacy pattern.

Try this with other geometric shapes.

This exercise is very easy to translate into fabric by using fine cotton treated with Bondaweb. Fold in eight and hold securely with paper-clips or pegs. Cut into the folds of the fabric. Apply the pattern by ironing to a background.

Close woven fabric like organdie can be sewn to the background or caught between transparent fabrics.

## DESIGN BASED ON THE ENVIRONMENT

### COLLECTING IDEAS

**1. Drawing** Much of the design work described so far, has been on using cut paper patterns and mathematical shapes. Appliqué is often concerned with making pictures as well as creating patterns, so it is useful to draw simple shapes and patterns.

Concentrate on drawing the outline shape and pattern of any object that interests you and that you might want to depict.

Make a record of the colours you can see, trying to relate these to your collection of fabrics.

**2. Cutting out** When you have drawn an object, place the drawing to one side and cut out the same shape free-hand in paper or fabric. This should be the same colour, as near as possible, as the predominant colour of the object. Look carefully at the object before you cut, and keep looking at it as you work. Affix cut-outs to a sympathetic background to make a design. Keep in mind your collection of fabric, thinking of that which will most nearly give an impression of what you have recorded.

*Sailing boats. Applied shapes on strip patchwork background*

**3.  Tracing and photocopying**  Photography is a quick way of recording, although nothing really replaces drawing. The ideal is to draw small areas of whatever is photographed as a back up. It is also useful to record colours directly from life.

Some photographs can be reduced to basic shapes by tracing off the main areas and leaving out detail. This can also be done on a black and white photocopier by enlarging the photograph to the size you want and then tracing off areas of texture and pattern.

Leaves, feathers and even slices of fruit (protect in a plastic folder!) can be photocopied and enlarged.

## THE MAN-MADE ENVIRONMENT: SETS AND COLLECTIONS

Man-made designs are often concerned with the arrangement and packaging of units. A multi-storey building is a package of flats or offices, a wall is an orderly collection of bricks or stones, a knot garden is a pattern of individual gardens, and a farm landscape is an arrangement of interlocking fields and woods.

Window-panes, floor tiles and walls are all individual units packed together to form a whole. They make a grid pattern, a patchwork, which is easy to reproduce because the unit shapes are so simple.

For example, you might take photographs and draw a variety of walls. Note the shape and size of each brick or stone in relation to its neighbour.

Notice flaws in the shapes. What overall pattern is made? Is the material used textured or patterned? What colours can you see?

**Other man-made objects**   Many are also based on grids and can be used as a design resource.

Look at the variety of windows. These are made more decorative and individual by the number and shape of the window-panes and glazing bars, window-boxes, balconies, creepers, washing and so on.

Even quite ordinary, everyday objects, e.g. books in a bookcase, jars on a shelf, stacks of goods in a shop, boxes of fruit in a market, make highly decorative patterns and pictures.

The arrangement of similar unit shapes and the patterns they make is more important than the detail. An appliqué is usually very impressionistic, relying on shape, colour and pattern to create the effect.

*Italian Cathedral by Mig Holder. Machine appliqué using dyed, painted and transparent fabrics and hand made paper.*

*Arched windows. Machine appliqué with machine embroidered flowers. Fabric pastel crayon background.*

Collect sets of objects and record them by drawing or photography.

Make pictures and patterns by cutting out unit shapes and sticking them onto a background.

As you work, notice how different they look:
1. from the front, looking straight on;
2. from an angle, when all the shapes are changed.

It is much easier to look at groups of objects straight on but some unusual almost abstract patterns can be produced by looking at collections from different angles.

Abstract patterns can also be made by looking at just part of a drawing or photograph with two pieces of card cut at right angles to form a window.

Draw or cut out what you can see, however strange it might look. Try to forget what you are looking at and think of it as an abstract shape.

## THE NATURAL ENVIRONMENT

There are many natural objects which are easy to reproduce because of their simple shape. Fruits, pebbles, and shells can be drawn or photographed and cut out. Look carefully at the object rather than trying to remember what you think it looks like.

WHAT TO DO
1.  Draw the shape of a fruit, a fungus, a shell or any natural object.
2.  Cut or tear the shape in fabric or paper. Match the colours carefully.
3.  Arrange these in a naturalistsic way, as if they were on a plate.
4.  Cut or tear the same shape in different colours, e.g. black and white, just one primary colour, all tints, all shades, etc.
5.  Arrange a number of the same shape, in patterns like those described on page 79.
6.  Try the shapes against different background colours.

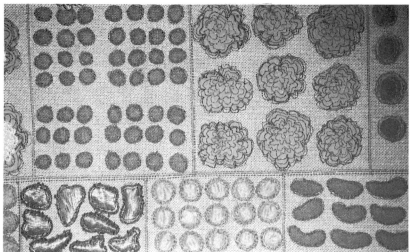

*Machine embroidered applied fabrics on paper backed hessian*

### Sets of natural shapes

Flowers appear complicated, but on closer inspection each individual flower is often composed of several similar shaped petals, arranged in a characteristic pattern.

Look at a particular flowerhead.

Make up a flowerhead from cut or torn coloured paper or fabric.

Cut out or tear unit shapes and make: a bunch of grapes, a pineapple, a tree, a branch of leaves, a pine cone.

Look for other complex natural objects which can be broken down into simple unit shapes. The individual scales on fish and reptiles, and the feathers on birds are not complicated in themselves, but only appear complex when they go together to form an interlocking pattern.

Keep going back to the original, making certain you have captured the basic shape, the correct colours and pattern. At the same time, collect fabrics which are as near as possible to what you want to create.

### Figures:
Do not be afraid of trying to depict human figures. The shape, rather than the detail is important.

Observe, draw, cut out, notice how joints will only bend certain ways and the proportion of each limb in relation to the others, etc.

People who are interested in dressmaking often make figures by cutting out garment shapes and dressing a stick figure.

'Créativité et Liberté by Alison Harding. Appliqué wall hanging in wool with various applied fabrics. Leather letters.

**Silhouettes**

Strong back lighting can change detailed three-dimensional objects into flat cut-out shapes which are ideal for appliqué.

Buildings and trees against the sunset, a group of figures against the sky or the light shining through a stained glass window make dramatic pictures. The effect of fog and mist is to blot out detail, leaving only outline shapes.

## MAKING A WORKING PLAN

To create a successful appliqué, every idea has to be reduced to a working design which consists of shapes glued on paper with added details of proposed colour, texture and pattern.

1.    Reduce the design to simple shapes. This can be done by tracing off the main areas of drawings, photographs and photocopies.

Look at the design in terms of areas of colour and tone, or of pattern and texture. Each area will eventually be a fabric shape. You can add details later or choose a fabric which provides an impression of detail in its pattern or texture. A drawing, collage or cut-out is always easier to interpret because these techniques simplify and abstract the parts you think are most important.

2.    Decide on the size of the finished work. An appliqué should not be too small or it becomes difficult to cut out the pieces.

3.    Enlarge or reduce the design to the correct size.

a.    Trace the design on tracing paper and divide into squares.

Select a piece of paper the size of the finished design and divide it into the same number of squares.

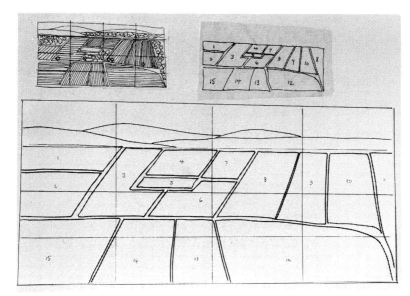

See p.25

Copy what you see in each square of the initial tracing into each square of the larger/smaller sheet.

b.  Use a photocopier to enlarge or reduce. If the projected design is too big, cut the tracing into smaller pieces, photocopy each and tape together. Large designs can be marked out on lining or shelf paper.

4.  Pin the design to softboard and stand back to look at it.

The design must be approved at this stage, otherwise it will be disappointing when finished. It might take quite a time to manipulate to your satisfaction, but keep working on it. Is it too large, or still too small? Sometimes the scale makes a difference.

You can break up very large areas with a mosaic of fabrics or fabric printing or stitched textures.

Keep this scale drawing as the master plan and trace off templates for the fabric shapes.

Keep all the other plans and designs, as you might need to refer to them.

**Choosing fabrics**  Think of what each shape represents. Think of the colour, texture and pattern. Is the fabric suitable for what you want to do?

Make sure the fabrics look good together.

Remember to think of the function of the finished piece when choosing both fabrics and background.

*The background might be:*

a.  just one piece of suitable fabric.

Will any of the background show and if so, how will the colour react with pieces of applied colours?

'American Election'. Machine appliqué
on patchwork background.

Any fabric can be used which is suitable for the effect you want to create ranging from a heavy canvas to a flimsy net.

Choose the strongest fabric available in a suitable range. Woven fabrics do not stretch, but in any case, a backing prevents this.

Flimsy opaque fabric can always be strengthened by tacking to a layer of calico or sheeting, with the straight grain of the fabrics running in the same direction. For a more transparent effect, catch the pieces between two layers of transparent fabric, sewing each in position.

Interfacing is also available in different weights from light to very heavy. Choose a suitable weight. As interfacing has no weft or warp it can be laid in any direction.

Paper-backed hessian (wallpaper) can be used for large pictures with many applied pieces. Paper can be glued to any fabric to create a background (see page 38).

b.    a patchwork of joined fabrics or of fabric strips.

This might also need the support of another fabric or interfacing.

The background should have a border of spare fabric all the way round.

**Sewing shapes to the background**    This can be done in a number of ways, or a mixture of several different ways. Choose whichever is most suitable.

The weft and warp of the applied shape should lie in the same direction as the background wherever possible. This keeps the work flat.

Otherwise, back the shape to be applied with iron-on interfacing or Bondaweb. In some cases even this is impossible and it is worth having wrinkles and a beautiful effect.

WHAT TO DO

1.    Cut out simple shapes with a seam allowance. Pin to the background. Turn in the edges and mitre the corners. Hem by hand or stitch by machine. This is most suitable for fine woven fabrics such as cottons, fine wool, silk, etc.

*PVC and silver foil applied to velvet. Straight stitch decoration.*

2. Cut out the exact shape and hem or machine to the background. You can leave a raw edge, which can look effective and delicate. Alternatively, the edges can be covered with hand stitches, for example couching, feather stitching or chain stitching. A close zigzag or a fancy machine stitch can also be used.

3. The whole design can be drawn out on iron-on interfacing. Cut out each piece and iron onto a suitable piece of fabric, leaving a seam allowance. Alternatively, cut out to exact size so the pieces fit like a jigsaw. Zigzag stitch, or cover the edges with hand stitchery.

4. Cover the back of the fabric from which the piece is to be cut, with Bondaweb. Draw the shape on the paper backing, cut out and iron on. Save the spare pieces with Bondaweb backing for later use. The Bondaweb keeps the applied pieces in position and stops them from fraying. Instead of sewing round each shape, make stitch patterns by hand or machine, catching in the applied pieces as you go. These stitch patterns might make vertical or horizontal lines or both, or they might follow the line of the shapes. The stitches should be used to enhance the applied pieces. Use straight machine stitches, free machine embroidery or hand stitches.

5. A mosaic of many small pieces of fabric might be lightly glued to the background, then machined all over. All sorts of different fabrics can be used successfully.

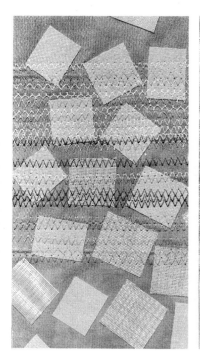  

*'Garden at Parham' by Vicky Lugg. Fabric mosaic with machine stitching pattern.*

6.   Fabrics which do not fray can be attached with just a couple of stitches so they hang away and create a three-dimensional effect.

7.   Flimsy fabric shapes can be held between two pieces of organza, tulle or net. Stitch round each with running stitch or machine.

### Reverse or inlay appliqué

This is a method of inlaying one fabric in another.

To try this you need two rectangles of different coloured cotton (15cm square). Lay one on the other and draw a rectangle on the back. Stitch round this with a sewing-machine using straight stitch. Cut the top fabric back to the rectangle. Turn and cut out within the rectangle to the stitches. Satin stitch all the way round.

Many beautiful effects can be created with this method, using a combination of fabrics like silk and net, satin and metallic, felt and wool and so on. Free machine embroidery with straight stitch can be used and several layers of fabric can be machined at the same time, then layers can be cut away to reveal those underneath.

This is only a guide to what might be done. The method or combination of methods depends on the fabrics and how you want the finished piece to look.

# FINISHING AND MOUNTING

Patchwork and appliqué are techniques which are suitable for large, dramatic areas of colour like church vestments, hangings, pictures, and stage costumes, as well as for garments and furnishings. However, the techniques are equally suitable for tiny and delicate pieces of work. The finishing makes a great deal of difference to the appearance of the work and it is worth spending time in finding a method which shows it off as well as possible.

## PICTURES AND WALL-HANGINGS

Decorative pictures and panels can be mounted and/or framed, or finished in a number of ways.

The work should first be pressed on the reverse side or through a piece of cotton sheeting.

### Lacing

Cut hardboard or strong card to the exact size of the work (excluding spare fabric at the edge). Cover this with a layer of wadding, lightly glued to the surface. Cut the spare fabric round the work to 5-6cm all round. Turn in the edges and machine to give a strong edge. Pull the fabric evenly round the hardboard and lace across the back starting in the middle and working to the sides.

In some cases the fabric can be glued instead of laced, but be careful not to get adhesive onto finished work.

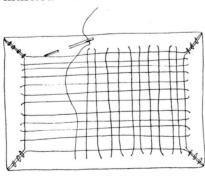

## MOUNTING

WHAT TO DO
1. Lace or stick the work round card, or stick the work to stiff card using double-sided Sellotape. This should only come in contact with the spare fabric round the edge of the work.

91

Mounting board is available in different colours. Choose a colour which looks best with the picture or pattern. Cut the board to size, then work out the dimensions of the inner edges of the mount on the reverse. Insert a pin through at each corner. Cut the card on the right side with a sharp craft knife, joining the pin holes. Mount over the picture.

2.    A picture can be laced on card and fixed onto mounting board. In both cases work can be framed and/or glazed in the usual way.

3.    Fabric can be laced or stuck round hardboard or soft board to make a mount. First attach two curtain rings to the back of the board to be used as hangers. Drill two holes a third of the way down the hardboard and 5 or 6cm in. Take a length of strong twine round each ring and cross the back. Knot securely. The work can then be laced on card and glued or sewn onto the covered mount. A piece of work with fringed or fancy edges can be sewn directly onto the mount.

4.    Small and delicate assemblies of fabric can be put between glass and fabric-covered hardboard in clip frames.

5.    Commercial frames are often quite cheap and can be utilised for pieces of work of suitable size.

## WALL-HANGINGS AND QUILTS

Patchwork and appliqué are often used for wall-hangings and quilts and these are both constructed in a similar way. Quilts are usually padded for warmth and body, and wall-hangings can be padded or interlined with heavy interfacing to give weight where necessary.

*'Pandora's Box' by Alison Harding. Patchwork hanging using silk fabrics.*

92

## Borders

Wall-hangings and quilts almost invariably have a border which not only finishes off the work, but sets off the patterns and pictures.

A border can be made of deep or narrow strips of fabric in contrasting or matching tone. Patchwork often has a patterned or toothed border. These borders can be attached by first sewing strips across the top and the bottom and then the opposite sides.

Alternatively, the corners can be mitred.

Some appliqué pictures or patterns might be finished by fringeing out the edges. Choose a border to match the work.

## Wadding for quilting

This is available in various weights and fibre types. Terylene wadding is washable. Cotton wadding is folded and should be opened and used with the fluffy side to the top. Fabrics like blanket can also be used as wadding.

Most people find 2oz weight wadding most suitable and manageable for quilts.

## Methods

There are a number of methods, of which this is only one.
1.  Lay the top fabric face down on a flat surface.
2.  Cut the wadding to fit the work. Strips of wadding should abut without spaces. Lay the wadding on the back of the work.
3.  Cut a backing fabric the same size as the work. This should match in with the patterned front, in colour and in type of fabric. A made-up fabric like strip patchwork can be used or the work can be double-sided.

Lay the backing right side up on the wadding, making sure all three layers lie straight.
4.  Starting in the middle, pin and tack the three materials together, making sure they stay flat. It is important that the pinning and tacking is strong enough to hold the layers together to stop them from shifting, particularly during machining.

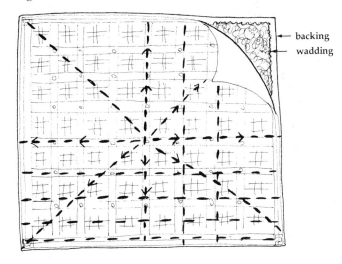

backing
wadding

93

*Hexagon cushions, positive and negative.*

## Quilting

The quilting stitches hold the three materials together and should be evenly distributed across the work. They can be worked in either lines or patterns, or ties can be placed every few inches apart. The lines of stitches should not be so close as to flatten the characteristic quilted texture, but not so far apart that the texture is lost.

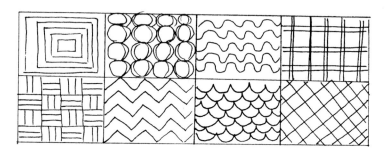

It is possible to work on a quilting floor frame, but these are rather large. Large quilting hoops are available and work can be done area by area. Many people manage to quilt on a large flat surface, or quilt small pieces in squares which are then joined.

Straight machine or a running stitch can be used. Work on the right side, from the middle outwards wherever possible to avoid inadvertent wrinkles.

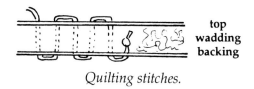

top
wadding
backing

*Quilting stitches.*

94

## Binding The Edge

Cut strips of fabric on the cross. Join a strip down one side by putting the right side of the strip to the right side of the edge and machining.
Repeat down the left side, then across the top and bottom. Alternatively, mitre the corners.
Turn the strip to the back and hem or machine.

## Alternatives

1.   A method which avoids binding the edge entails cutting the backing fabric approximately 2.5cm larger all round, than the work itself. The bottom fabric can then be turned over onto the front to make a hem.
2.   Lay the work face down and tack the wadding onto the back of this. Cut a backing the same size and place the work and the backing right sides together. Machine all round, leaving a slit for turning. Turn right side out and pull straight. Tack and quilt as above.
3.   If you are working in multiples of squares or strips, quilt and back each square individually. To join these, place two squares right side together and stitch along one edge. Join the squares to form strips and join the strips. The backings can then be overlapped and slip stitched as you go along. Quilt along the seams.
4.   Tack wadding to the backing fabric. Strips or squares of patchwork can be added one at a time. Start in the centre and work out, adding strips by placing each right side to right side, machining and turning, so each overlaps the one next to it.
5.   Make individual blocks, quilt and bind, then join.

## WALLHANGINGS

These can be made so they are supported right across by making a tube or sleeve of matching fabric to hold a dowel or rod. Cut a strip of fabric the correct width to hold a dowel on the straight grain of the fabric. Turn in the edges and tack, then tack across the backing. Use either hem stitch or running stitch to hold the sleeves in position.

Alternatively, a strip of Velcro can be stapled to a wooden batten screwed to the wall. The matching piece of Velcro can be stitched to the back of the work.

## CUSHIONS

The making of cushions is an easy and quick process.

The top should be the same size as the cushion pad. It can be quilted simply if necessary, before making up. If the work you want to use is too small, add a border.

The backing should match the cushion. If the cushion is reversible, the opening should be at the edge.

**Openings**   Allow enough spare fabric to make an opening. Let in a zip-fastener before sewing the back to the front. The work can then be turned through the open zip.

*Log cabin cushions by Roberta Warren. Quilted transfer printed motifs.*

A suitable opening can be made by making the backing in two pieces and overlapping by approximately 4 or 5cm. Press-studs or hooks give added support.

If the opening is at the edge, it can be strengthened with bias binding, sewn on and turned onto the wrong side.

WHAT TO DO

The backing and the top should be of the same size. Work the openings, then lay the top and backing right sides together. Machine, rounding the corners very slightly. Cut across the corners for a crisp finish. Turn through the opening.

Large stores like John Lewis plc stock fabrics, instructions and templates for patchwork, and fabric dyes and paints.

Consult Yellow Pages for:

Art and Craft Shops which stock dyes and fabric paints with instruction books and leaflets. Some of these also stock patchwork fabrics, and templates, books and leaflets.

Many fabric retailers now stock American craft fabrics for patchwork and appliqué and numerous relevant books and leaflets.

## Books and resources

Many local museums have historic examples of patchwork and appliqué. The American Museum in Britain, Bath has a superb collection of quilts, and an extensive Bookshop, including their own publications:

## Useful books:

| | | |
|---|---|---|
| Quilts and Coverlets and | Sheila Betterton | The American Museum in Britain |
| More Quilts and Coverlets | Sheila Betterton | The American Museum in Britain |
| 101 Patchwork Patterns | Ruby McKim | Dover Publications |
| The Standard Book of Quilt | | |
| Making and Collecting | Marguerite Ickis | Dover Publications |
| Fabric Printing for Embroidery | Valerie Campbell Harding | Batsford |
| The Textile Design Book | Karin Jerstop | |
| | and Eva Kohlmark | A & C Black |

Look also for simple maths and pattern books like:

| | | |
|---|---|---|
| Polysymetrics - the art of | | |
| making geometric pattern | June Oliver | Tarquin Books |
| Draw patterns | Anna Brockett | A & Black |

Mail order suppliers and details of courses and classes can be found in the small advertisements in the following publications:

The Quilters Guild Magazine. PO Box 66, Dean Clough, Halifax, Yorks HX3 5AX

Needlecraft, Future Publishing, Freepost, Somerton, Somerset TA11 7BR

Embroidery Magazine, PO Box 42, East Molesey, Surrey. KT8 9BB